TOUCHING

the

FIRE

Also by Ray González

TOUCHING

the

FIRE

FIFTEEN POETS OF
TODAY'S LATINO RENAISSANCE

Edited and with an Introduction by
RAY GONZÁLEZ

ANCHOR BOOKS/DOUBLEDAY *New York London Toronto Sydney Auckland*

AN ANCHOR BOOK
PUBLISHED BY DOUBLEDAY
a division of Bantam Doubleday Dell Publishing Group, Inc.
1540 Broadway, New York, New York 10036

ANCHOR BOOKS, DOUBLEDAY, and the portrayal of an anchor
are trademarks of Doubleday,
a division of Bantam Doubleday Dell
Publishing Group, Inc.

Book design by Leah S. Carlson

Library of Congress Cataloging-in-Publication Data

Touching the fire: fifteen poets of today's Latino renaissance /
edited and with an introduction by Ray González. — 1st ed.
p.   cm.
1. American poetry—Hispanic American authors.   2. American
poetry—20th century.   3. Hispanic Americans—Poetry.
I. González, Ray.
PS591.H58T68   1998
811'.54080868—dc21   97-28949
CIP

ISBN 0-385-47862-3
Copyright © 1998 by Ray González
All Rights Reserved
Printed in the United States of America

First Anchor Books Edition: February 1998
1   3   5   7   9   10   8   6   4   2

CONTENTS

~~

JUAN DELGADO

MARTÍN ESPADA

DIANA GARCÍA

GLORIA VANDO

TOUCHING

the

FIRE

INTRODUCTION

≈

As we approach the new century, Latino poetry is in the midst of its most vital and productive period. Its writers have been key factors in the larger gains Latino literature has made over the last twenty years. Poetry by Mexican Americans, Puerto Ricans, and Cuban Americans has changed the course of contemporary American writing forever. It has done this by emphasizing poetry as the sound of everyday life— showing readers and other writers that the most effective manner of preserving the traditions of a culture, while evolving in a modern world at the same time, comes from the colorful language of daily experience. Latino poetry has returned emotion and spirit to a genre that had distanced itself from its readers by an overemphasis on objective experimentation. Most important of all, its poets have played an important role in bringing growing, literary audiences and communities together.

Touching the Fire recognizes this environment by focusing on a few of its major poets. By presenting a substantial portion of each poet's work, this book stands out from the dozens of anthologies of Latino literature. Literary success has meant wider publication and an energetic push to get many good collections of Latino writers into more hands. While this has resulted in a rich variety of titles, many anthologies have included dozens of poets with two or three poems each. Generous inclusion has served the purpose of introducing many established and younger poets, but it has not allowed the careful reader to get to know key individuals from the crowd.

Touching the Fire honors fifteen poets who are making important contributions to the field. Some of them have been writing and publishing for a long time. Several poets are younger writers starting their careers. All were chosen because they best represent the strongest aspects of Latino poetry—a confidence of language in its many forms, a gift for shattering, emotional honesty, and an ear for the rhythms of a vibrant culture.

The ten poems by each poet represent new and old work. Some of the selections are taken from important, past books by writers with long careers. A number of the poems are appearing here for the first time. The creation of fifteen mini-books in one amplifies the style and voice of each poet. The fifteen poets stand alone, in their own distinct manner. Together, they celebrate the complex character of Latino writing, which is a vibrant and moving literature that will be among the first to be read as the literature of the Americas influences how all of us step into the next century.

SANDRA M. CASTILLO

LETTER TO YENI ON
PEERING INTO HER LIFE

I see you, not as you stand before me,
so full of language threatening to spill from you,
a silver-blue luminous substance the page of cups
might carry in love, in a gold chalice,
but as a child I might have seen, held,
had I been an adult on that island
where we might have become anyone
other than ourselves.

You are a sound you say your father carries,
a beat in the heart of an African drum
that seduced him with the thunder of *Changó*
the red of blood and earth,
a flesh-pink guava growing inside you,
its seeds on the tips of your fingers
like islands, like memories becoming leaves,
their veined undersides becoming maps,
palmlines, bridges where the sound of water collects childhood
in a blue bucket of memory,
where my Tío Machuco stands with childhood sandwiches I ate
sitting on the cold *terraza*, leaning against the Southwest red
of that couch Tía Hilda discarded like a useless memory
when we were no longer voices in open rooms with connecting
doors,
when we were words, onion-skinned paper
as transparent as re-written history or exile.

ALMENDARES

⌘

for Tía Estela

Blood puddles on the Spanish white floor
like a secret no one talks about
though every one feeds it, like imagination,
with hushed conversation translating into fear,
into memories I am told were never real
though rooms roared like the morning lion
that hid in the closets of the upstairs house you rented
to a woman who couldn't understand
why dawn found her undergarments scattered on the steps
of her life, a display of familiarity or intimacy,
and patterned echoes yawned like voices trapped between the
clavicles
of the past where opaque breaths,
calling us to maids quarters long sealed,
sounded like the wind between the caves of the underworld
we thought would swallow us
into darkness we opened looking for sounds,
for hands folding into knocks,
for mouths moving into vowels, words,
for someone invisible who woke you to midnight weight
pressing upon you with the invisible thrust of unfamiliar desire
until you could feel nothing running between your legs
but the invisible moving inside you
and a hot breath, never your own,
equaling pain, diving fear into stories
that kept us looking for what we never found.

PRIMOS

❧

Time is the longest distance between two places.
— TENNESSEE WILLIAMS

You are in Camagüey when we arrive,
twenty-five years after we left you,
a summer in Artemisa: your eyelashes,
silk calligraphy, batting letters,
long glances of blue becoming
an island sky, a childhood photograph your mother,
Tía Hilda, will show me
the day before we leave La Habana once again
as if to remind me
that neither time nor distance
can snap the invisible balance
of familial recognition
the night my displacement will frame *el apagón*
with the ebb and flow of circumstances,
with the candles we light to see the *picadillo*
you and I will purchase on the southside of the island
in an American grocery like the ones Tío Berto dreamed
when living in the U.S. was still ninety miles away
and Tía Hilda still thought we were wrong to leave.

Heat settles like nostalgia on my forehead;
I wait to see you, for I do not know what to imagine
until Tía Hilda shows you, adult you, to me:
black and white, glossy, portable you,
someone unfamiliar smiling in my hand
thick with questions, assumptions, erasures.

It is February, I think.
Late afternoon sun spills

over your left shoulder,
your black sweater.
Trapped by geography,
you lean against a 1955 Ford Fairlane,
an odd, leftover 50s we never knew,
out of time, out of sequence.

I hold you a long time,
and though she is mouthing words,
spinning sentences into the aftertaste of absence,
it is today and water surrounds us,
separates us, moves between us,
her ambient voice, our homesky,
and I am trying to run through my childhood to find you,
to make out the color of your eyes,
the shape of your fingers, our sameness,
the patterns of our veins beneath what is real,
but there is no language.

And I wonder what might happen
if, *parentesco olvidado*,
I were to think your lips
the mouth of the sky,
your halo-being eyes, fixed stars,
Japanese lanterns, and if caught breathless
by the arch of your brow,
I'd want to wear your kiss,
for I know there are still spaces,
slots between who we are and what we live
where words end, where language seizes
to encase us in the folds of her untouched skin,
in her blue backroads, her slender capillaries
and the pale light of forget
flirts into love.

MONDAY NIGHT AT PEDRO'S

∾

for A.

Pedro's mother greets us on the street,
calls us *"Mariconas,"* says we've left the gate open,
says Napoleon, Hitler and Fidel could have escaped,
says we're *"Locas, periodistas locas,"*
like my camera scarred me, named me
extrañamente in this achromatic city
of flaking stucco and vintage America
where Mother and I walk towards Avenida Real
with strangers meant to be family,
where I hold my cousin's hand,
think of cornerless strangeness,
optical double stars, random moments,
Schopenhauer, unknowable things,
a four-letter abstraction
because this is the first time
we've ever seen one another
and surely, family is ritual and familiarity,
practice and indoctrination,
a psychological phenomenon that escapes me
though Mother asks if I've gone mad
this night we sit among the white *mariposas*
in Pedro's yard, the moon watching,
and hiding.

THE CONTRA

∾

I don't recall his name,
only the slits of his eyes.
We found him on your front step
after dinner, a walk on pastel-colored South Beach,
the deco district.
It was your day off.
We had run home to be naked, alone,
to lie under your ceiling fan,
your long hair on my face.
With legs propped up on your balcony
on the second floor, he waited,
his black leather phonebook
on his military lap.

He wore a yellow *"Don't Worry,*
Be Happy" t-shirt and he spoke about me
as if I wasn't in the same room.
"Where did you find *this woman?*" he'd ask.
Interspersed with laughter,
this later became a response to questions
he couldn't answer.

Turning his Spanish into English,
we learned you had shared a major,
yours in Tel Aviv, his, Ft. Bragg, special tactics.
And though he had to say *"Tell him this. Tell him this,"*
he never looked me in the eye
because, he said, I wasn't a man.

He said he needed a place to sleep in Miami,
and he had been given your name.
You fed him the tabuli we had both made

and waited for his words to become English,
your second language.

All night, I tried to be your dictionary,
but my words turned into questions
he couldn't answer and my mind became a third world country;
dark-haired, outdoor-skinned men in military green
lined the Honduran border like thick, leafless trees,
their M-16s on tight shoulders.

I heard gunfire, saw the night turn to blood
as it filled my lungs,
felt the wind come off the ocean,
pound on the windows of your studio apartment,
wrap itself around my neck
like night or death.

AT THE HAVANA HILTON

A speechless moment thins my blood;
I am a line in my hand, a name,
my mother's name, my father's name,
a white house on a street that never changes.
The fragments of my heart lost
in liquor or self-indulgence,
I read your eyes like Tarot cards.

Unaware of words that fall
into blood and murmurs:
my love, my love,
I hold myself out to you, My Hang Man,
like a tinted glass of afternoon,
where you remain, suspended in a chrysalis.

Across the street of want,
the Communist-red signs
of a Chinese restaurant bleed
anonymous, infinite.
In a dream, or awake, love is a continent,
and pain, like distance, is as red
as the neon that flashes and pulses,
like my heart, into the sky above all of this—
This is a map. This is my life.
"Un poquito de aquí. Un poquito de allá."

And I want to be your Magician,
fly you over the deepest moat
across stretches of salt and strangeness
to the southern tip of this, my life,
stitch heaven and earth and air,
and wear infinity like a hat,
but the past is a stubborn stone.

EN EL SOL DE MI BARRIO

for Reinaldo Arenas

I.

Fourteen years after you snuck
onto a boat *en el puerto del Mariel,*
I think of you in this place of pilgrimage
prayer and lamentation, Reinaldo Arenas,
desperation under your fingernails
like the red clay of earth
you used to lick
collecting Cuba inside you
one inch at a time
until she was an island in your throat,
a tapeworm you had to expel
from your body.

You are here, Reinaldo,
en el sol de mi barrio,
a stressmark on the tanned skin
stretching over the tenuous bones of island boys
collecting, like sweat and despondency,
en los portales de La Habana,
where they gather to stoke an amorphous dream
of Miami *con chispas,* a blaze,
a flash of pyrotechnics,
liquid insanity with salt and lemon.

You linger in corners,
where the past ferments,
floats inside my head like an incandescent buoy,
flotsam, jetsam, chance,
irregular circles patterning the darkness,
this island night, the southern hemisphere

with constellations: Perseus, Cassiopeia,
Scorpio, Sagittarius, The Southern Cross,
stars your grandmother could name
on this leather black evening as anonymous
as an unfamiliar body,
as intimate as an old lover.

2.

Sunstruck,
I drive past La Concha,
afraid of the past,
the subtractive properties
of convenient memory.
Children gather by the entrance of my childhood
with black innertubes,
with eight years of Sundays
my Sundays: my mother, my father,
my fear of depth and breathing and water and sinking
like a stone though I fight for that memory
and yours intrudes.

Were you ever here with me,
in this place I thought my own?
Did you wade in these waters,
next to my mother, smile at my father,
make him an asterisk in your life
while I shivered in the darkness
beneath an empty sky?

I remember the jade green changing rooms,
a sight of privacy you sprayed,
leaving yourself here,
impervious to time I choose not to look at
in this exile of subjectivity.

Think of it, Reinaldo:
Time is curved, a circle, a halo,

and we, we are abstract nouns, verbs,
here, *en nuestra ciudad*, La Habana,
where we meet, linger, float into ourselves
with our waterwings:
island to dream
dream to island,
because we are water,
somos agua, Reinaldo,
and time is a Gypsy,
un brujo extraño que mendiga
en la esquina del pasado.

RINCÓN

We curve along the edge of civilization:
overgrown canefields, sombreroed men
with saffron skin and machetes
lining the road we share with farm equipment,
tractors, ox carts, and those who dare
to bicycle the island with children
strapped to homemade wooden seats
with hope for a Sunday *paseo*
un día cenizo y triste que se sienta
en mi garganta como un licor extraño.

And you, a product of the revolution,
my cousin, my brother, my love,
have learned to live with horror,
con dolor y escasez, con tus ojos tristes,
and the sixteen-hour night you chase
back to Habana in this choleric air
that blows through the open windows
to touch our shoulders and lick our lips.

It has taken me twenty-five years
to get here, to feel these sunburned vinyl seats
stick to my tourist skin with the adhesive that is sweat,
to hold your child who jumps over the dampness
settling inside us, this car,
while you, fascinated by speed and geometry,
spiral through this ash-gray Sunday,
the confused impurity of my thoughts
as your son reaches for his toy alligator,
a Florida souvenir.

EL APAGÓN

for A.D.

It is my last night in Havana,
and childhood fills me like the moon,
her slow arc, her seraphic light, our only light,
illuminating my hands, your eyes.
Blindfolded by *el apagón* that dresses the island,
we drive down Avenida 89, the geography of chance,
looking for ice,
the pavement disappearing under us,
the darkness swallowing the blackened streets.

And I am eight years old again:
my eyelids are filled with sweat and breath
and salt and night,
and I am choking on twenty-five years,
squinting for words that might direct us
to a place unspoken
where all side streets lead us
to who we have always been,
to where there are more reasons
to remember than to forget,
to where we don't drive past ourselves
missing something we cannot name
or identify.

Trapped in time, in a tape you find me,
because I say the 1970s were a sad song
whose title I never recall,
because certain lyrics negate memory,
shaped by water and distance,
because music makes our ordinary lives one,

La Formula Quinta sings to us:
"_. . . Hace frío en mi alma, ya no puedo pensar . . ._"
to an old life that remains a witness,
that pulls me here, an unsuspecting corner
where you park, trade a favor for ice,
for a good-bye that will fill us
with the _chispas_ neighbors will bring
when the Havana Club runs into midnight,
when you pull me aside to tell me something
you never say,
when the night disintegrates,
becomes an uncertain blue,
dawn, the moment I leave.

CUBA

⚬⚬⚬

Night is everywhere. In the bars of exclusive hotels, she is Mount Olympus, The Abode Of The Gods, a note, a flute, a golden laurel, Castalia, Delphi's sacred spring, a banquet of grace and muse, Ambrosia, The God Of Wine, *un respiro, un beso,* a festival in a tight black dress, a lady finger, a cherry bomb, *tambor y son,* a lira, a Dutch mark, an American dollar, a witch whose silver earrings glow like phosphor, firelight, *un cigarrillo,* a flashbulb, a mirrored ball or the ice encased, encircled in her humid hand, a Gipsy, a moon-faced lover who knows how to *salsa* across your skin, *merengue* over sleep and memory to lodge herself between your shoulder blades like desire, The Lady Wild, Artemise, Diana, Goddess Of Youth, Cupbearer to German tourists who drive along the edge of the island, El Malecon, in the comfort-safety of air-conditioned Mercedes with tinted windows and smiling cab drivers who play "I'm going down in a blaze of glory . . ." for them, the tourists, the visitors, the honored gods who think themselves *isleños* with a Cuba Libre, a Macanudo, a *guaguancó.*

In Marianao, she is formless darkness unbroken, mad melancholia, black-winged, circles, spheres, the spinning wheel of chance, curved lines into La Pollería, Isaac's Mercado, empty tin cans, anonymous and mysterious, lining the shelves where history hides, like a rat, waiting to be absolved; she is Dementer's grief: barren earth, seedless and dry, a suffering god, Prometheus bound and chained to misery and a rock, a vulture feasting on his liver, *Masetas, Chivatos, gineteras, El Comite,* marriage proposals from passersby, a shapeless mass of nausea, grief, infernal heat, incandescent ash and smog, the odorous fumes of *luz brillante,* feces, urine, sweat and decay, garbage and curbside maggots, gnats, mosquitoes, *cucarachas,* lice, parasitic worms charmed out of the body by heat and dysentery, potholes, coal-black chasms, fractures, fissures, a buffet of *apagones y escasez,* an old woman on Avenida 89 taking to the streets, an empty *olla* in her hand, exploding *cafeteras* across La Lisa, a mixture of chick peas and coffee beans dripping down kitchen walls, a fifteen-year-old girl in a cobalt-blue dress selling herself for *"fula,"* *Granma* inklines, black smears on private skin, bloodstained rags clotheslining misery across the island like a river of lamentation and woe, The World Beneath The Earth, The God Of Fire, Hades, Lord Of The Underworld, King Of The Dead, a three-headed dragon-tailed dog at the gate of Hell.

In Artemisa, she is a serpent, a burrow, a cave, a black spot, a by-stander, voiceless anger, lamed and deformed, *el hambre de una isla,* Io tied and stretched, the raw, connective tissue of thirty-five years of The Brazen Age, the acrid buffet of calamity, the bowels, prostration, *vinagre y muerte,* a duststorm, a firebox, a muletrain, a ground mine, a labyrinth, Pandora's box opened, *un río de enfermedades:* Amblyopia, Anemia, Tuber-culosis, Hepatitis, Meningitis, Optic Neuritis, dysentery, Eris, Goddess of strife, guilt and blame, the ruthless fury of a militarist, an inflexible god, a punishing god, a beast god, a Centaur, a Satyr, a Fury, a Chi-mera, Nemesis, Fidel wreathed with serpents, a dragon-like creature with wings and a look that could turn you into stone, into Atlas, sentenced to bear the vault of the sky, the immeasurable chaos of a crushing world alongside Sisyphus who rolls his rock through Artemisa, Phaeton's world on fire: furnace air, sulphur flames, burning ash, the afterburn, the bloodsmell, the wounded, like Dyonisis, torn to pieces, a sacrifice, or into Hercules combating the preposterous mon-sters of a revolution's imagination: bread lines, news lines, medicine lines, innertubes, *la escuelita,* The Black Market, a broth, a barter, *un apagón,* farm animals in the livingroom, the theater of the absurd, the fear of death and starvation, Ché and Revolutionary Square, his severed hands with Fidel, whose house lights the distance between Heming-way's Marina and Santa Fe, whose land gives birth to *plátanos, tomates, lechuga, mangos, guayabas, zanahorias, malangas,* and beets while the spirit of the dead, *cadáveres dormidos,* lounge in Villa Miseria and Saturn devours his own children.

Lorna Dee Cervantes

THE POET
IS SERVED HER PAPERS

So tell me about fever dreams,
about the bad checks we scrawl
with our mouths, about destiny
missing last bus to oblivion.

I want to tell lies
to the world and believe it.
Speak easy, speak spoken to,
speak lips opening on a bed of nails.

Hear the creaking of cardboard
in these telling shoes?
The mint of my mind
gaping far out of style?

Hear the milling of angels
on the head of a flea?
My broke blood is sorrel, is a lone
mare, is cashing in her buffalo chips.

As we come to the cul de sac
of our heart's slow division
tell me again about true
love's bouquet, paint hummingbird

hearts taped to my page.
Sign me over with XXXs
and *passion*. Seal on the lick
of a phone, my life. And pay.

And pay. And pay.

THE LEVEE:
LETTER TO NO ONE

∞

Today I watched a woman by the water
cry. She looked like my mother: red
stretch pants, blue leisure top,
her hair in a middle-age nest egg.
She wiped her face, her only act
for old tears, slow as leftover piss.
She was there a long, long time,
sitting on the levee, her legs swinging
like a young girl's over sewer spew.
She slapped her cheeks damp.
I wondered what she watched:
blue herons, collapsing and unfolding
in the tulles, half lips of lapping river
foam, the paper of an egret's tail?
Does she notice beauty? Does she notice
the absence of swallows, the knife
of their throats calling out dusk?
Does she notice the temporary
denial of fish, the flit of silver
chains flung from a tern, the drop
of their dive? Funny, we use the sound
slice to imitate the movement
of hunger through wind or waves.
A slice of nothing as nothing
is ever separate in the realm of this
element. Only symmetry harbors loss,
only the fusion of difference
can be wrenched apart, divorced
or distanced from its source.

I walked the levee back both sides
after that. The river is a good place
for this silt and salt, this reservoir,
depository bank, for piss
and beauty's flush.

AN INTERPRETATION OF DINNER
BY THE UNINVITED GUEST

In the evening dusk when earth
is half star, half rock of red light,
when heaven opens to let out her crew
of white, bread-cheeked angels, marching
on to moral wars,
at six, exactly, the family
sits to supper. I watch them
in secret from my second floor apartment.
All hands, I see a Punch and Judy
farce: the right and left take turns.
The window is their stage. They perform
for me, alone. They pass. They set.
Their pats of butter, stewing
the tears from the fleshy buns;
and finally, they settle their places,
unfold their napkins, and begin
the feast.

I am alone and hungry
and I watch this every night
from my voting booth room.
If I turned on the light
they would see me. But I never.
The hands would reattach themselves
and who knows what country
their bodies dwell in.

STARFISH

∾

They were lovely in the quartz and jasper sand
As if they had created terrariums with their bodies
On purpose; adding sprigs of seaweed, seashells,
White feathers, eel bones, miniature
Mussels, a fish jaw. Hundreds; no—
Thousands of baby stars. We touched them,
Surprised to find them soft, pliant, almost
Living in their attitudes. We would dry them, arrange them,
Form seascapes, geodesics . . . We gathered what we could
In the approaching darkness. Then we left hundreds of
Thousands of flawless five-fingered specimens sprawled
Along the beach as far as we could see, all massed
Together: little martyrs, soldiers, artless suicides
In lifelong liberation from the sea. So many
Splayed hands, the tide shoveled in.

TO WE WHO WERE
SAVED BY THE STARS

∽∘∾

Education lifts man's sorrows to a higher plane of regard.
A man's whole life can be a metaphor.
— ROBERT FROST

Nothing has to be ugly. Luck of the dumb
is a casual thing. It gathers its beauty in plain
regard. Animus, not inspiration, lets us go
among the flocks and crows crowded around
the railroad ties. Interchanges of far away
places, tokens of our deep faux pas, our interface
of neither/nor, when we mutter moist goodbye and ice
among the silent stars, it frosts our hearts on
the skids and corners, piles the dust upon our grids
as grimaces pardon us, our indecision, our monuments
to presidents, dead, or drafted boys who might have
married us, Mexican poor, or worse. Our lives could be
a casual thing, a reed among the charlatan drones,
a rooted blade, a compass that wields a clubfoot
round and round, drawing fairy circles in clumps
of sand. Irritate a simple sky and stars fill up
the hemispheres. One by one, the procession
of their birth is a surer song than change
jingling in a rich man's pocket. So knit, you
lint-faced mothers, tat your black holes
into paradise. Gag the grin that forms
along the nap. Pull hard, row slow, a white
boat to your destiny. A man's whole life
may be a metaphor—but a woman's lot
is symbol.

ISLA MUJERES

∽∾∾

pa' Javier

There's an arch in your heart,
a deserted landscape languishes
steeped in the weight of the sea.
Waiting. Enough of the coral
sand, white elephant sheen,
my pelvis pressed between the pages
of your knees. In the cavity
wind bows through, that part
of you that never stays
like the fixed portions of a blown
through past, I can not change
an absence that is
a space, a whistle-whittled
pain, or ever wish it. Just long
Mayan paths to trace, my indigenous
toes starched with salt, my *Purépecha*
spine erect, ignorant of your long-gone
sex. My brown dog stirs, agitates,
displays. I think I'm a part of you
but it's only celestial, nothing
reflecting the blue. If you were
a man like a rock you could fill,
stave, remember: how our poverty
sticks, how a spirit saves, how frank
the powers are in the ancient
sprays, the perfumed rock, a ruined
sun and the devil wind; a matrimony.

A UN DESCONOCIDO

I was looking for your hair,
black as old lava on an island
of white coral. I dreamed it
deserted you and came for me,
wrapped me in its funeral ribbons
and tied me in a bow of salt.

Here's where I put my demise:
desiring fire in a web of tide,
marrying the smell of wet ashes
to the sweet desert of your slate.
My intelligent mammal, male
of my species, twin sun to a world
not of my making, you reduce me
to the sick syrup of the moon, you boil
my bones in the elemental absence of hands.

Where is your skin, parting me?
Where is the cowlick under your kiss
teasing into purple valleys? Where
are your wings, the imaginary tail
and its exercise? Where would I breed
you? In the neck of my secret heart
where you'll go to the warmth of me
biting into that bread where crumbs crack
and scatter and feed us our souls;

if only you were a stone I could
throw, if only I could have you.

ON THE POET COMING OF AGE

for Jim Harrison

there was this poet
                              with a wandering eye
                    he was cool
I was a street kid
                    a moving   sheet of ice
                         a floe   a cipher
no moon
                    the street lamps aired a golding
    sulfur   my skin
              gilded
              and the satin   skirt   I was naked
under
                         swept mooned shells
              of light through the glassed asphalt
seventeen   and nobody's girl
         96 pounds of bad
                              burning
                              the midnight
                                        barrio
         oil   lit
                    a ticking flint
he sat at the Five Star bar   reading
         Rupert Brooke   or Lowell
    how
         little now
                         I remember
              just the smoked pool of light
how he
         (not the half-blind poet   but the other
                              almost man)

                    sat
                           squinting at the leaves
of verse   I recall
                              how he cradled the stump
                        in the pouch
                    of his demin   but not
        his name or the face
                    just a beauty   the blank
                        backlit page
                    my bustless boldness
never replaced   or ever
                        recaptured
                              how I leaned
                    on
        the bar stool
                        radiating and   irradiating
                    the sullen drunks
                    the demeaning mouths
    a field   a force   there
            parroting passages of Baudelaire
                        Rimbaud
                        Vallejo
                        youth
                    remembering   youth
        in   those   years   I   owned
                    whatever I touched
                    whatever I said
he was another hemisphere   a continent   divided
        by a man   made canal   no side
                    could claim
        he was a poet   from the midwest
                    he'd come
                    to read Brooke
                              or Lowell
at the U   which I knew   was a lie
            the jolt
that woke his flesh

                    was not the fire
                                    bird
        hand-painted on satin
    nor my wild flight
                            of hair
                                but the English
    I spoke
                    the enunciated
                                    unexpected
    Cool   I said
                and made a date for the Greyhound
                    knowing he'd go
                    cruising for a better   lay
                    but when money
                    and beauty failed
                                        to pay
                I took him & his wall-eyed friend
            back to my condemned   Victorian
        there are these ships   see   you can   sail
                without   course
    an expanse of ocean crossed on a dare
        choice isn't limited
                    to Sartre and Simone
                it's a game   the poor play
                            at wit's end
    it was a game
    out   guessing   out   reciting
    out   smarting   the   legitimate
                and the boy I took to bed
                        was
                                    sexed
    when he undressed
                    my defeated city
            he took what could have been a fist
                from his pocket
                            the stump
            glowing milk in the smoking light

                    his gnawed-off paw
when I touched it he was soft
                        thin
                                        a woman
            in a man a girl could love
he put it out of sight
                            If thine hand offend thee . . .
and with a tenderness for an absence
I both felt   and did not
    I make him   rise
                                        swell   cliff
                                    sail

                        Fucking poets
he breathed in the candle dark
                    as I tunneled
                    in all ways
                    that can be
                        taken
                    whispered
                multi   pieced
            lean as pricked goose meat
in the morning
the poet left by cab
I walked the boy to the bus
barefoot through the glass
pissed winoed streets   the other
        left a poem about Mexicans
                                    depots
                            and the sullen poor
                    all gone
I read it and researched
my 17 hungered years in the mirror
        and I dare it to say it
                I am a poet

FIRST BEATING

〰

What a strong little sucker you are!
All my grit and guts rolled up in a fist.
All I ever had was strength: head
strong, heart strong, even my genius,
tempered, impermeable: all my soggy wishes
hard-boiled away early, nothing but blades
of glass in the end, fused to the bottom
of my past, bitter crystals shimmering, and
there for good.

   From these damaged goods,
I pass you the flame, my ware. Alive
in your sea of blood and spit and piss
your ventricles unfurl, hurl into space
like the hands of maize, the thick pricks
of daffodils asserting through the wimpy dirt.
You beat a good goddamn through the conjugal
mush, up between the aged cracks in my skin,
through my pores I hear it rapping: first poem,
first flush of wings and separation. You give
me this: a heart like a jackhammer tearing
up my world. Oh my little secret weapon, self-
made slayer, you are mine. My strength. Your own.

ARCHEOLOGY

I can't keep my hands from stones,
rocks of another age, chipped obsidian
blades, jagged monsters etched in sea
jade, graying zebras of hieroglyphs,
small black eyes of agate, saved
Indian signs chiseled from my kin. I rise
with the weight of loaded-down pockets;
all you buried treasures like a loose
hard-on knocking against my thigh, an old
woman's jewels in her empty house, a womb
alone in the pouch of my flesh.

   Here's for you
to find: a comb with a few silver threads,
a map to the caves where the spirals
of heaven print scarves on the shale, where
digits of splayed testimony plant their red
mark upon the diamond granite, where the older
bloodstone, sand-dappled, reveals the ravaged
river shrimp; here in the brine of history
and the pulverized bone, I find my sinker,
discover the leaden lure as ancestral
graves give out; and I endure.

JUDITH ORTIZ COFER

THE CHANGELING

As a young girl
vying for my father's attention,
I invented a game that made him look up
from his reading and shake his head
as if both baffled and amused.

In my brother's closet, I'd change
into his dungarees—the rough material
molding me into boy shape; hide
my long hair under an army helmet
he'd been given by Father, and emerge
transformed into the legendary Che
of grown-up talk.

Strutting around the room,
I'd tell of life in the mountains,
of carnage and rivers of blood,
and of manly feasts with rum and music
to celebrate victories *para la libertad.*
He would listen with a smile
to my tales of battles and brotherhood
until Mother called us to dinner.

She was not amused
by my transformations, sternly forbidding me
from sitting down with them as a man.
She'd order me back to the dark cubicle
that smelled of adventure, to shed
my costume, to braid my hair furiously
with blind hands, and to return invisible,
as myself,
to the real world of her kitchen.

SAINT ROSE OF LIMA

＠

Never let my hands be to any one
an occasion for temptation.
—ISABEL DE FLORES

She was the joke of the angels—a girl
crazy enough for God

that she despised her own beauty; who grew bitter herbs
to mix with her food,

who pinned a garland of roses to her forehead;
and who, in a fury of desire

concocted a potion of Indian pepper and bark
and rubbed it on her face, neck, and breasts,

disfiguring herself.
Then, locked away in a dark cell,

where no reflection was possible,
she begged for death to join her with her Master

whom she called *Divine Bridegroom, Thorn*
in My Heart, Eternal Spouse.

She would see His vague outline, feel His cool touch
on her fevered brow,

but as relief came, her vision would begin to fade,
and once again she would dip the iron bar into the coals,

and pass it gently like a magician's wand over her skin—
to feel the passion that flames for a moment,

in all dying things.

THE PURPOSE OF NUNS

As a young girl attending Sunday mass,
I'd watch them float down the nave
in their medieval somberness, the calm
of salvation on the pink oval of their faces
framed by tight-fitting coifs. They seemed above
the tedious cycle of confession, penance
and absolution they supervised: of weekday dreams
told to a stranger on Saturday; of Sunday sermons long
as a sickroom visit, and the paranoia of God always
watching you—that made me hide under my blanket
to read forbidden fictions.

Some of us were singled out for our plainness,
our inclination to solitude, or perhaps—
as our mothers hoped in their secret hearts—
our auras of spiritual light only these brides
of quietness could see in us. We were led to retreats,
where our uninitiated footsteps were softened,
and our heartbeats synchronized, becoming one
with the sisters'. In their midst, we sensed freedom
from the worry of flesh—the bodies of nuns
being merely spirit slips under their thick garments.
There was also the appeal of sanctuary in a spotless mansion
permeated with the smells of baked bread, polished wood
and leather-bound volumes of only good words.
And in the evenings, the choral mystery of vespers
in Latin, casting the final spell of community over us.

The purpose of nuns was to remind us
of monochrome peace in a world splashed in violent colors.

And sometimes, exhausted by the pounding demands
of adolescence, I'd let my soul alight
on the possibility of cloistered life, but once the sky
cleared, opening up like a blue highway to anywhere,
I'd resume my flight back to the world.

WOMEN WHO LOVE ANGELS

⚬⚬⚬

They are thin
and rarely marry, living out
their long lives
in spacious rooms, French doors
giving view to formal gardens
where aromatic flowers
grow in profusion.
They play their pianos
in the late afternoon
tilting their heads
at a gracious angle
as if listening
to notes pitched above
the human range.
Age makes them translucent;
each palpitation of their hearts
visible at temple or neck.
When they die, it's in their sleep,
their spirits shaking gently loose
from a hostess too well bred
to protest.

THE CAMPESINO'S LAMENT

It is Ash Wednesday, and Christ is waiting
to die. I have left my fields dark and moist
from last night's rain, to take the sacrament.
My face is streaked with ashes. Come back,
Mujer. Without you,
   I am an empty place
where spiders crawl and nothing takes root.
Today, taking the Host, I remembered
your hands—incense and earth, fingertips
like white grapes I would take into my mouth
one by one.
   When I enter the house,
it resists me like an angry woman. Our room,
your things, the bed—a penance
I offer up for Lent. Waking with you,
I would fill myself with the morning,
in sweet mango breaths. Watching you sleep,
I willed my dreams into you.

But clouds cannot be harvested, nor children
wished into life.

   In the wind that may travel
as far as you have gone, I send this message: Out here,
in a place you will not forget, a simple man
has been moved to curse the rising sun and to question
God's unfinished work.

LAS MAGDALENAS

While it's still dark,
they drape shawls over their sequins,
swing black-stockinged legs
out of long cars parked a block
or two away. The five A.M. mass
is preferred, convenient.
   On entering the dim nave
they begin to shed *la vida:* stale
perfume absorbed by the censer
the angelic altar boy swings
as he leads the sleepy man
in scarlet robes—no less splendid
than the women's evening clothes—
to the altar—the man with the soft hands
who does not touch women, the one
who can drive the money changers away
from the temples of their bodies.
   Each Sunday it is the same,
like sweeping sand from a house on the beach.
They bow their heads to accept
what was promised Magdalene.
The tired man serves them humbly
at his master's table. He breaks the bread
and pours the inexhaustible wine.

"Peace be with you." He sends them away
an hour before dawn. "And with you,"
they reply in unison, yawning
into their mantillas, ready now
for the clean sheets of their absolution.

THE LESSON OF THE TEETH

I heard my mother say it once
in the kitchen—that to dream of teeth
means death is coming, rattling
its bag of bones as a warning to all
to say a "Credo" every night before sleeping.

One day, as a child, seeking the mystery
of my Aunt Clotilde's beauty,
I slipped into her bedroom without knocking.
She was sitting at her vanity,
combing her long black hair everyone said
I'd inherited. A set of false teeth
floated in a jar beside her. In horror,
I looked up into the face of a sunken-cheeked hag
in the mirror—then ran all the way home.

She must have seen me but never let on.
Her face filled with flesh appeared often
at our place. But her smile
sent a little current of icy fear up my spine—
that message they say you receive
when someone steps on your grave.

MY GRANDFATHER'S HAT

∽◦∾

in memory of Basiliso Morot Cordero

I cannot stop thinking of that old hat
he is wearing in the grave: the last gift
of love from his wife before they fell
into the habit of silence.

Forgotten as the daughters chose
the funeral clothes, it sat
on his dresser as it always had:
old leather, aromatic of his individual self,
pliable as an old companion, ready to go
anywhere with him.

The youngest grandchild remembered
and ran after her father, who was carrying
the old man's vanilla suit—the one worn to *bodas,*
bautismos, and elections—like a lifeless
child in his arms: *No te olvides*
del sombrero de abuelo.

I had seen him hold the old hat in his lap
and caress it as he talked of the good times
and, when he walked outside, place it on his head
like a blessing.

My grandfather, who believed in God,
the Gracious Host, Proprietor of the Largest Hacienda.
May it be so. May heaven
be an island in the sun,
where a good man may wear his hat with pride,
glad that he could take it with him.

ANNIVERSARY

❦

Lying in bed late, you will sometimes read to me
about a past war that obsesses you;
about young men, like our brothers once,
who each year become more like our sons
because they died the year we met,
or the year we got married
or the year our child was born.
   You read to me
about how they dragged their feet through a green maze
where they fell, again and again, victims
to an enemy wily enough to be the critter hero
of some nightmare folktale, with his booby traps
in the shape of human children, and his cities
under the earth; and how, even when they survived,
these boys left something behind
in the thick brush or muddy swamp where no one
can get it back—caught like a baseball cap
on a low-hanging tree branch.

   And I think about you and me,
nineteen, angry, and in love, in that same year
when America broke out in violence
like a late-blooming adolescent, deep in a turmoil
it could neither understand nor control;
how we marched in the rough parade
decorated with the insignias of our rebellion:
peace symbols and scenes of Eden
embroidered on our torn and faded jeans,
necks heavy with beads we did not count on
for patience, singing *Revolution*—
a song we misconstrued for years.

Death was a slogan
to shout about with raised fists or hang on banners.

But here we are,
listening more closely than ever to the old songs,
sung for new reasons by new voices. We are survivors
of an undeclared war someone might decide to remake
like a popular tune. Sometimes, in the dark, alarmed
by too deep a silence, I will lay my hand on your chest,
for the familiar, steady beat to which I have attuned
my breathing for so many years.

THE LESSON OF THE SUGARCANE

My mother opened her eyes wide
at the edge of the field
ready for cutting.
"Take a deep breath,"
　　she whispered,
"There is nothing as sweet:
Nada más dulce."
　　Overhearing,
Father left the flat he was changing
in the road-warping sun,
and grabbing my arm, broke my sprint
toward a stalk:
"Cane can choke a little girl: snakes hide
where it grows over your head."

And he led us back to the crippled car
where we sweated out our penitence,
for having craved more sweetness
than we were allowed,
more than we could handle.

VÍCTOR HERNÁNDEZ CRUZ

KEEPING TRACK OF THE SERPENTS

～○○～

This is what will happen
This is what will go down
This is what you been thinking about
What last night's dream was planting
This is what has been written
By drops of water at the tips of tree roots
This is what you been trying to decipher
This is the secret of the rocks
This is it:

Near the center of the earth
Circulate huge reptilian snakes
The size of the Lexington Avenue
Subway Express
Thousands of them
With faces the size of cars
Amazing
Add to that the fact that
Their faces are human
And their hair neatly combed
In a twist

Their appearance is what's going
To go down next
Wham! no matter where you live
Eating pork chop in a slum
Or caviar in Hollywood hills
When you see it your eyes will be
In Cartoonland
As they pop to where these
creatures surface
In the commotion that will

Follow
Some will run for their dictionaries
Others will go for their zoological books
Many will go for their Bibles
Since taking pictures with cameras is in
You can imagine the rush for the film
The churches will be packed
As will be the offices of scientists
Talking about
We must get a hold of it
We must name it
It's gonna be like wow name that shit
The military will go for their heat

But wait
This is what has been written
This is what's in the tablets
Endlessly and has come down to this
Shock which has popped
This huge snake with a cute old face
An hour or more after their appearance
The legend starts churning
Not only do they dive in and out the
Water with their strips of primary colors
They zoom off into the air
And start to orbit clouds
The scientists munch on their brains
The christians are confessing like birds
The air gets full of flute sounds
Above the snakes like gypsy scarfs
Spinning washing machine the air
Colors are fruits for the eyeball
Mouth

It's all over, some say
Even the hustlers give up their
Circle

This has got to be it
No the phenomenon keeps weaving
The huge flying snakes
Turn the sun off and everything is
Black until they turn their lights on
And they are moving rainbows
Now get a hold
Even your feet start to dream
That the sidewalks commence to
Dance and wax the whole earth up
Like a glass
This human-faced snake
Next starts to excremetize
Greenish pink bubbles
Coming down on your head
To shampoo your pendants

As it was written that it will
Manifest itself
When this number 56,979 will talk
As it is in the codices
As it is known in the stars
What the waves of the ocean scribble
This is what will happen
This is what will go down
This is it

SNAPS OF IMMIGRATION

❧

1.

I remember the fragrance of
the Caribbean
A scent that anchors into the
ports of technology.

2.

I dream with suitcases
full of illegal fruits
Interned between white
guayaberas that dissolved
Into snowflaked polyester.

3.

When we saw the tenements
our eyes turned backwards
to the miracle of scenery
At the supermarket
My mother caressed the
Parsley.

4.

We came in the middle of winter
from another time
We took a trip into the future
A fragment of another planet
To a place where time flew
As if clocks had coconut oil
put on them.

5.

Rural mountain dirt walk
Had to be adjusted to cement
pavement
The new city finished the
concrete supply of the world
Even the sky was cement
The streets were made of shit.

6.

The past was dissolving like
sugar at the bottom of a coffee cup
That small piece of earth that
we habitated
Was somewhere in a television
Waving in space.

7.

From beneath the ice
From beneath the cement
From beneath the tar
From beneath the pipes and wires
Came the *cucurrucu* of the roosters.

8.

People wrote letters as if they
were writing the scriptures
Penmanship of women who made
tapestry with their hands
Cooked criollo pots
Fashioned words of hope and longing
Men made ink out of love
And saw their sweethearts
Wearing yellow dresses
Reaching from the balcony
To the hands of the mailman.

At first English was nothing
but sound
Like trumpets doing yakity yak
As we found meanings for the words
We noticed that many times the
Letters deceived the sound
What could we do
It was the language of a
foreign land.

ISLANDIS

This is the taste of the
Guavas of Hesperides
That converted a *sabor*
Of eyes on loan from the sun.

Was the Carib isles
The ink in the plume
Of Plato—
In the philosopher's mind
A sandy curve of coast
Stretching into red soil
And sky out into the lamps
Of the Gods.

Mayagüez plain Maya
Before the Castillian Güez—
Yabucoa the town's name is
Singing
A stepping stone to Atlantis—

Spectacular ships entered
The domain of Humacao
Guided by red corals
And the incense of gold
Navigational songs of the nymphs
Spiraling out of sea shells.

Were the *coquís* ten times
Louder in age remote
Could they have been
The singing notes
That drove Homer's sailors mad.

Did someone speak of Anacaona's
Hairdo of braids weaved
With gardenias
In some Roman antiquity of
Córdoba—

Let us bow our heads
In silence
Pushed back to the twilight
Of ideas
And with the next Venusian
Light to telegram into
Manatí
Declare ourselves
The kings and queens
Of Poseidon
Wearing crowns of
Bird gone feathers.

SCARLET SKIRT

I terminated with the color red
when this vibrant hue pressed against
me up on a mountaintop
Upon which I didn't know how I got
Drunk and in pursuit of a scarlet
skirt that had made a passage through
a festive plaza
It started the way it started
but don't ask me how that was
Rum and 98 degrees is a devastation
of the senses
Through her lips she gleamed a yes
And with that yes we went off on
a journey onto a street to the point
where cement ran out
And the red dirt began
The night was choking the daylight
out of the atmosphere
You could still count the *coquís*
which had started their nightly
Glee club
We didn't hold hands
But in the sway of the walk our pinkies
would brush against each other
In midair
She told me her name but it was
already the point when the bottle
Of rum was beyond the halfway mark
So all I could do now is speculate
Was it Nilsa, or Elena or Julia
Just plain and thrown
Or was it Ana-María, Sonia, Carmen
Something with more combustive

Syllables
Or was it a much more rural name
Like Blasina or Amparo
It is all now in the flow of the
river that we might have passed
En route towards a singular light
At the very top of the earth
Which was her house
This part of the path was full
Of rocks which turned out to be
frogs
For they would take leaps
In front of my foolish head
Which by now had more rum
Than the bottle
The sounds of animals
The soft breeze
The crescent moon
Convinced us to sit on a
fallen tree
Her legs dispersed out of
her scarlet skirt in various
Curves
As we spoke little episodes
of our histories
I shot flurries of warm moisture
into her ears
And then as quick as a lizard's
head she stood up
Saying I must go
disappeared into the darkness
The tail of a cow which had
been watching us from a distance
Did more than us
There I was in the sullen shade
of night holding an empty
Bottle of rum far from the

center of town in an elevation
Which I knew not
Composing myself I threw the bottle
away and took direction
My head in the misty heaven of
sugar cane
Singing the opening lines of one
bolero after another
Lo I came upon a fork in the road
Going is never like coming
A pause of indecision
The whole Caribbean stood still
I just went in the direction I heard
less frogs and *coquís*
Thinking myself en route towards
civilization
After some paces I found the hole
of my life
I fell down a precipice like
a clown in a movie
With my white apparel I cleaned
the side of the mountain
And fell into a gathering of
guava bushels
There I was drunk and dizzy
crimson from the mud I had
Rolled on
I shitted twice on the cipher 10
and continued my journey into
Town
At long last I found the lights
of the beginning
Soon I was crossing the plaza
It must've been one in the morning
I looked like a potato that had
been internalized in a pot of
Red beans

I made a turn on the street
leading to my home
Suddenly I saw a figure of
good dimensions standing next
To the gate
It was not human but a beast
I came a little closer and
registered that it was in fact
A bull
Tremendous bullshit
I found a rock and threw it in its
direction to see if it would scatter
Away
But it was immobile
It just stood there waiting as
if I owed it some money
I had to find an alternate way
of getting to my bed
I went through a side street
and climbed the stairs of
Don Berencho's house which gave me access
to the roof of the house next to
mine
This put me in jumping distance
onto the back balcony of my house
I swore that I had left the door
open
Once I jumped and turned the knob
it told me something else
It had been closed
I thought of yelling to my sister
But I reviewed my condition
Drunk
Bumps and scratches all over
And my clothes looked as if I'd
just climbed out of a pot of
Red beans

What words could be occupied as
an explanation?
I laid myself out on an old
rattan sofa that we had there
The thought of the scarlet skirt
beat me to sleep
It is such an expensive color
it's the heat of our passions
I terminated with the color red
After descending from the
mountaintop.

NEW/AGUAS BUENAS/JERSEY

In the forties the populace was sucking on barb
wire
Cans found on the streets were squeezed to the
maximum
Hot air moving through wooden houses
They were Bohíos
We were Tainos
It's Areyto moving down from Sumidero
Pouring in from Caguitas
Inside the living rooms Aguasboneses walked
on compressed dirt
They made it shine
Cooked on kerosene stoves
Says the elders they woke up with stained noses
The chemical odor did them in
For that reason they lived in the streets
They lived in the mountains
Go home to eat and sleep
Roosters mounted chickens at random under
houses
For the children the toys were the insects
and sing songs from the time of Spain
Closer than Spain was the pain
People survived with the beauty of the song
The hidden gracious heart
That love that loved whoever it was
We carry our blood
Even towards destructions
And what else could it be
An army to fight destiny: for what in the matter
The families collapsed like red flowers
off of *flamboyán* trees.

The Spanish wanted gold first.
The priest wanted converts.
Sailors have always wanted pussy.
The Taino kingdoms melted in the mountains
The Areytos into the bone marrow to mix with
The juices of semen to that now generation
Our faces aboriginal designs

The island was purgatory
The retina saw in flora and fauna the spirit half
The same way a chest or a cross is visible
It was our materialism
The Spaniards came with so much embroidery
Our virgins were naked
This is a climate for flesh
Up in Mula thrown on a hammock receiving wind
upon my testicles
Aroma of *azucena* jumps only at night
The same as La Siciliana who only opens
within the darkness
In the eyes of the plaza I can still
see the nakedness pouring out
The heat invites us to take off our clothes
Imagine such polyester melted by the
primal sun

I am moving in the tensions with the tenses
History hanging within long skirts
The Black Virgin La Montserrate on a passage
Through the center of a town of wooden
Houses painted blue, green, yellow, pink,
orange
Black shawls and white hats
Join the rivers, the trees, the frogs,
and the rain which is about to fall
And the rain which is about to fall

Rain
In adoration of an image

The island was abandoned by history
Only the sun fell upon a coast of Sourtern
Spaniards who improvised a government
Accusing others of the crimes they committed
To settle Taino yucayeyes they went deeper
inland
With flashes of Moorish and Visigothic
harmonics
Made paths through the guayaba flavor

Avicenna and ibn 'Arabi in costume at the
festival Bomba y Plena
Pineapple in Baghdad Morocco

The silence of the past
Rules the manifestations of the future
The spirits are in charge here
Who comes through Guánica
Who comes through San Juan Bay
Who comes through airport
Doesn't know how ridiculous
the riddle can get

The space was exported
as industry was imported
The campesinos were taken into the future
There was only past and future
There was no now
The Marine Tiger left
Sumidero Mula Caguitas
La Pajilla El Guanábano
went to Newark Avenue
Bergen Montgomery
Grove

Sixth Street
There was nothing to do in Aguas Buenas
But to stare into the mountain Jagüeyes
There was no government
No plans for agriculture
The plans were for tourist
and pharmaceutical companies
The people who dropped the bomb on
Hiroshima came from the North
The methods were different
but the clearing was the same
A beautiful house with no one in it

Jersey City take the path back
To the island of vegetation
Let us retrogress into the future.

LA MILAGROSA

As red as her lips were she wasn't there
The lonely night like a hidden moon crater
Which wouldn't be there if it were not for eyes
So look at the assembly of fire escapes
High up like on some kind of Ferris wheel
Hearing now footsteps inside the wax of the
Candle which burns for La Milagrosa
Go down the street to see *maniobras*
On the way back the gargoyle that protects
The entrance started talking:
The tops of heads have clear holes
I been spitting rainbows into them for
100 years tonight the half-baked moon
Is there I can breathe it with my nose
Which says the moon is full every day
All the time the moon is out and all
There full like your head in a dream
Close the windows
Aren't those the words of a song humming?
The street turns into soup
Her lips kiss the candle's fire
She walks open my walls
The sky is what I eat with my mouth
Virgin of the Miracles makes a
Sandwich of me between the sky
And the moon
Loneliness is yesterday's newspaper
She pokes her fingers into the silver
Holes of stars
Celestial orgasms like squeezing
Pluto-size cherries over a lemon earth
Roses clean their feet with the face
Of the gargoyle which looks onto the stoop

As red as her lips become blue
Like the mouth of an Alaskan glacier
La Milagrosa leaves footprints on my mind
She leaves stains on the goatskin drums
She leaves the odor of wax
She leaves the fire burning
She is gone from where she never came to
What you hear is only the song maker's
Humming
The street is deserted and covered with ice
The ice that used to be fire

THE ART OF HURRICANES

Out of Africa arises a silence
To dance with the sky—
Spinning it makes its music in the air
Follows the route of the drum,
Comes towards the Atlantic—
To drink rum in the tropic islets
To use the bamboo as flute.

Big horizon of space upset,
Traveling through moisture and heat,
It has been known to throw steps
Of 176 miles per hour—
And still as yet a man of the mountains
Observed a miniature orchid
Purple and yellow
Hold on with such a pride
That it withstood the hurricane—
To hang with the Christmas flora,
Months later in our hot winter.

Each Hurricane has its name
Its own character—
Hugo was strong and clumsy,
His strokes were like Van Gogh—
Bold and thick.
Pellets that were punches against the doors.
He came in spirals-vortex.
Painting the sky of *Starry Night*
Above us.
He was veritable like tropical fruit.
Devouring mangos and guava at will.
Breadfruit which flavors the tongues of Malaysia,

Enriching the waists of the hula dancers
In the South Pacific whose belly buttons
Hear better than ears.

Breadfruit which fries or boils
Was rolling through the streets
Of small towns surrounded by mountains—
Hugo as if it did the favor
Of going shopping for us
With free delivery.

The Lesser and Greater Antilles like
Keys on a saxophone
An acoustic shoot
Each playing their note.
Did he blow?
A high sea note
Crescendo-waves
Coastal blues.
An air of leaves,
A percussion of branches
In the melody
The sound of green.

As if an asteroid fell
From the heavens—
Making all the religious
Church goers
Hallelujah onto their knees
To pray in total fright
In the face of death,
As if all that church attendance
Was not enough
To give them the blessings
When finally God sent
An Ambassador in the form of a Cyclone.

Makes one see that
People act contrary
To the laws of science.

Iris was a bitch—
She flirted from Longitude 14
To the 19th—zig-zagging
Lateral West
Through spaces of latitude—
All that stripteasing
And she didn't come.
She went North,
Beautiful Iris
With her almond eye—
Full of lusty gusts.

Marylyn had curves—
A buttocky volution,
An axial memory that went down
To her tail.
At first she was a mere
Gyrating carousel on
The stage of the horizon—
On the satellite picture
She looked like a splattered
Sunny side up egg.
Her eye small
Like a black *frijol*
A beany socket,
Searching for the Virgin Islands.

Maelstrom of the sky—
A piranha of Caribe moisture,
Calypso in the middle eye—
A vision which is also breath.

A hurricane is the heart burn of the sky—
A schizoid space,

A rotating mill of nervous air.
What made it so worried.
How did it become so angry.
The atmosphere sneezes.
God bless you.

A necklace of *esmeraldas,*
The stairway of islands
We are sitting roosters
Waiting to be caressed
Our turquoise gown
Ripples in the wind.

Why was it that that Friday eve
When the hurricane was coming in
The Beauty Parlors were full—
Get dressed María
Permanent your hair—
Luscious Caribee—
Extra starch
Case I hang my head out
To the breeze tonight.
Sand, palm, white rum
And perfume. A band
Of clouds for white shoes.

The islands look like scattered spinach
That fell into a blender.
Whirlpool dancer
Licking the rim of the sun
Achieving the enlightenment
That comes through motion and moisture.

After Marylyn Saint Thomas
Was like a Jackson Pollock painting—
Telephone lines like a plate of Spaghetti.
A canvas of pickup sticks
Covered with random chance zinc roof sheets

Automatic rhythm art of happenings improve—
A colorful square of inspiration.

St. Croix was in the joy of Kandinsky's
Brush,
Lateral strokes pushing the sky
To collapse into molasses.

In the howling screech a thought:
Have the stars been blown away.

Caribbean islands
Sprinkled in the form
Of a crescent moon
Falling into Venezuela,
The land of Simón Bolívar,
The Orinoco
Currency of our blood.

A hurricane clears the earth's
Nasal Passages
A hurricane would do Los Angeles well—
The winds of Luis
Could have been packaged
In banana leaves,
Its eyeball of great
Cinematropic suggestion
Placed right outside Beverly Hills,
Driving through the freeways
Breaking the speed limit,
A vacuum of 100-mile radius
Dispelling contamination—
The picture in motion.

Tainos knew that palm Bohíos
Were portable homes—
When the tempest came

To remove them—
In two days they had them
Back up.

As the wind roars
Like a million ghosts—
Huracán's words accent each letter.
Goes through in total disrespect
Of industry and technology
And conventional itinerary,
Things disappear.

Hurricanes go west
Then north to be cool.
A spirit which knocked
Down Antillean coconuts
Could still be breeze
Cooling tea in Scotland.
My dear Lord—
What passes through
A fruit of passion—
To sniff along the English.

The horizon was a bowl
For Marylyn to make her stew—
Stir in the calabacín
The ocean soup.
Ancient appearance
Would have been
Below in caves.
Subterranean Church
Next to the hidden river
Flowing in peace—
Allowing the passage
Of Huracán—
Bowing in respect.

TWO GUITARS

∽∽

Two guitars were left in a room all alone
They sat on different corners of the parlor
In this solitude they started talking to each other
My strings are tight and full of tears
The man who plays me has no heart
I have seen it leave out of his mouth
I have seen it melt out of his eyes
It dives into the pores of the earth
When they squeeze me tight I bring
Down the angels who live off the chorus
The trios singing loosen organs
With melodious screwdrivers
Sentiment comes off the hinges
Because a song is a mountain put into
Words and landscape is the feeling that
Enters something so big in the harmony
We are always in danger of blowing up
With passion
The other guitar:
In 1944 New York
When the Trio Los Panchos started
With Mexican & Puerto Rican birds
I am the one that one of them held
Tight like a woman
Their throats gardenia gardens
An airport for dreams
I've been in theaters and *cabaretes*
I played in an apartment on 102nd street
After a baptism pregnant with women
The men flirted and were offered
Chicken soup

Echoes came out of hallways as if from caves
Someone is opening the door now
The two guitars hushed and there was a
Resonance in the air like what is left by
The last chord of a *bolero*

PERLAS

❧

pa' José Fuentes

The old men in the hills
say they shake the bottles of rum
to see if they have any pearls
They are bubbles that speak of the spirits
The longer they last
the better your drink
Good pearls will make you whirl, they insist
The earth is not straight
so why look at it that way?
If you walk on the beach late at night
The waves will not get you dizzy
if the spirits have your sight
Sunrise will find a string of pearls
around your head
Good rum must have pearls
That is good knowledge
That is something that you need

IT'S MILLER TIME

∽◦∽

I work for the C.I.A.
They pay me with cocaine
and white Miami sports
Jackets
Free tickets to San Juan
Where I make contact
with a certain bank
Official at the Chase
Manhattan bank

My contact a guy named
Pete asks if I know other
dialects within the Spanish
"Can you sound Salvadoran"
They give me pamphlets
along with pornographic mags
They got their hands in the
back doors of warehouses
If I want a stereo or a C.D.
a VCR
They could bring it all
at half price
Tickets to rock and roll
concerts
Where they drug the people
with lights.

The last assignment
I had was to contact
the P.R. division
Of a beer company—
Because for U.S. "Hispanics"

it was Miller Time
I contacted the brewery
A certain Miguel Gone-say-less
Invited me to lunch
That to meet him at La Fuente
Plush *frijoles*
Girls with peasant blouses
serving—
Low-key mariachi birdly
Community program directors
dining their secretaries
Big ole bubble of tie knots
Back at a table there he
was
Drinking Dos X's
and cracklin tortilla chips
With him was a Camden New Jersey
Cuban who was going through
Town en route to Los Angeles
the lunch was on them—
Senor Gone-say-less
Had credit cards thickly
He had more plastic than Woolworth's.

They mentioned that the
beer company wanted to sponsor
Salsa dances within the community
Bring in the top commercial
orchestras
. . . and that while this dance was
Going on they wanted to pass
a petition against U.S. involvement
in Central America—
They demonstrated the form some
organization they invented
Latinos Against Intervention
The petition had space for

the name and address of the
signers
A great list to have and share
around all government agencies.

They gave me a bag with three
thousand dollars in it—
It was my responsibility to
organize the petition circulation.
The Cuban guy tapped me on the
shoulder and said:
"Don't have any of the mixed drinks
the bartenders at the dance are
working for us, the chemical people
are experimenting the effects of
a new liquid just drink the beer."

The festive event was smashing
people were stuffed into a ballroom
The band smoked
The beer company gave out caps
Ladies dressed like Zsa Zsa Gabor
Romeos thrown back propped for image
Circling the ice of their Margaritas—
A full moon gleamed into downtown.

Next week the C.I.A.
is flying me back to the
Caribbean
where I will assist in staging
One of the strangest events in
world history,
According to the description we
are going to pull off a mock
Rising of land from beneath
the Caribbean
Which the media will quickly

identify with Atlantis—
Circular buildings made of crystals
are being constructed in Texas
They will be part of the
Espectacular
Which will have the planet
spellbound
Simultaneous with this event
the Marines will invade the
Countries of Nicaragua and
El Salvador from bases in Puerto Rico.

It will be a month of Salsa fest
in San Francisco
An astounding mystical event off
of Bimini
The price of cocaine coming through
Miami will drop
Everybody stunned party and
celestial
Glittering frozen and drunk
Circuits jammed with junk and
Information

In a daze of rapid commercial
flight
Colonialism and business
Mark their 500th anniversary
the world is free
It's Miller Time.

Signed: Double Agent El Lagarto

SILVIA CURBELO

PHOTOGRAPH OF MY PARENTS

I like the way they look together
and how simply her smile floats towards him
out of the dim afterglow

of some memory, his hand
cupped deliberately
around the small flame

of a match. In this light
nothing begins or ends
and the camera's pale eye

is a question that answers itself
in the asking. *Are you there?*
And they are. Behind them

the wind tears down and blows
apart, angel of nonchalance.
The world belongs to the world.

For years he smoked down to the filters
sorting out the pieces of his life
with the insomniac's penchant

for detail. In the heart's
heavy forest, the tree of self-denial,
the bough, the single leaf

like the blade of a word held back
for a long time. The moment
she leans towards him the room

will become part of the story.
The light is still as a pond.
My mother's blue scarf

is the only wave.

THE LAKE HAS SWALLOWED
THE WHOLE SKY

Some dreams are like glass
or a light beneath the surface of the water.

A girl weeps in a garden.
A woman turns her head and that is all.

We wake up a hundred times and
don't know where we are. Asleep

at the wheel. Saved by
the luck of angels.

Everyone touching his lips
to something larger, the watermark

of some great sorrow. Everyone
giving himself away. The way

the rose gives up the stem and
floats completely, without history.

In the end every road leads
to water. What is left of a garden

is the dream, an alphabet of longing.
The shadow of the girl. Perfume.

DREAMING HORSE

after the painting by Franz Marc

I could lie down in all that blue.
I'm watching shadows tell
their own story, a pasture
that sleeps through anything.
The voice is a meadow, the river
is a wing. I wanted
to be there so completely
I thought this poem was you asleep,
your quiet breathing.
So many words keeping track.
The heart is an odd museum.
Sadnesses display themselves
in corners, in rooms
as empty as this field.
The hand denies the face,
the past lingers.
I let my voice climb out
of my cold shoes. It talks
to air, it conjures
what it needs, a landscape
without blame, a room
the color of a whisper.
When I think about love crawling
through this world exhausted
with no place left to fall
I could run circles around
the word. I could say it
to anyone. Listen. Somebody
dreamed this.

TOURIST WEATHER

❧

All summer long hurricanes
with the names of movie stars
light up the weather map
across four counties. We drive
in silence out of the hospital
and towards the small strips
where souvenir shops with nautical names
are selling everything half price.

            ❊ ❊ ❊

Shells are bones. I've put on
your old raincoat. Whatever
plays on the car radio belongs
to the rain. Weather is the
only news worth waiting for.
Last night the young nurse
threw open all the windows moments
before the first storm hit
and through the trees we could hear
the coarse talk of the waves,
a language without tenderness.

            ❊ ❊ ❊

Driftwood, seashell, stone.
Some things are more
than their names.
Like hurricanes. Or cancer.
A word like that can kill you.

            ❊ ❊ ❊

A shell held to one's ear
tells nothing. Rain falls
between the cracks of what
we mean to say. Last night
I dreamt cool water filled my mouth
and my own voice, adrift inside it,
held itself up to you
like any human thirst.

DRINKING SONG

∾∾

after Schumann

In every half-filled glass a river
begging to be named, rain on a leaf,
a snowdrift. What we long for

precedes us. What we've lost
trails behind, casting
a long shadow. Tonight

the music's sad, one man's
outrageous loneliness detonated
into arpeggios of relief. The way

someone once cupped someone's
face in their hands, and the world
that comes after. Everything

can be pared down to gravity
or need. If the soul soars with longing
the heart plunges headfirst

into what's left, believing
there's a pure want
to fall through. What we drink to

in the end is loss, the space
around it, the opposite
of thirst, its shadow.

LISTENING TO A WHITE MAN
PLAY THE BLUES

∽∘∾

Pushing the seed into the ground
isn't enough. Whatever blooms

in this place is dumb and blind.
Foreclosure is a one-eyed man.

Nothing falls from a sky like this
except a little rain, never enough rain.

All night my wife looks down
the neck of my guitar

passing the bottle back and forth
like a story she's been telling for years.

So many baskets of hard bread.
You take the shovel to the ground.

The land stares back at you.
The corn drifts towards the sky.

You don't know what dirt is
until you bury your first daughter.

BEDTIME STORIES

✺

after Marc Chagall

Say it isn't real.
Say this violin is not a window.
The rose opening up from its shadowy heart
conceals its stupid thorn
like a child before his first mirror.
But a painting is not a mirror.
The colors are not real.
The flowers swaying in the hushed light
tell us a different story
and the child drifting through a landscape
of trees and numbers cannot hear it.

The trees are the one constant,
always touching the earth
but reaching for something else.
The violin itself is not color
but lightness. The music
rising beyond the highest
branches imitates flight,
sleep, a kind of floating.
This happens long before the idea
of falling enters the picture.
We attempt to grow graceful and weightless.
We leave our shoes behind.

This is the pure air of a painting
like a child before an open window
waiting for someone to begin
the next story, to bring him
his nightly drink of water

or lie beside him on the little bed.
The bed can be a mirror,
but not as real,
not at all like a painting
or a rose. His head resting
on the pillow is so sweet.
It could never be a tree,
it grows inward, rootless,
floating towards sleep.

Already we know this story
is not real, the colors
are too vague. The child
closes his eyes and imagines
the rest of his life
like a dream about falling
from a great height.
But this is early on,
before sleeplessness, before
he comes to terms with the idea
of gravity and the window
shuts completely in his dreams.
He will lose track of the story.
He will stare at the ceiling.
He will learn to count sheep.
This is a prelude to something else,
something that comes much later,
not sleep, but a kind of falling
through layers of himself,
not at all like a rose
but a sheaf of numbers
adding up to the one belief,
a feeling he can count on,
the pure mathematics of desire.

It happens slowly. He begins to see
himself in multiples of two,

of four, the world unfolding
in a graceful symmetry, two lips
two breasts, then his own longing
multiplying, becoming
a mirror to the girl
who is beautiful, who lies
in his two arms, who is
like a painting, or music
going on somewhere else.

This happens earlier,
before he learns to think in multiples
of three, before coming face
to face with his two hearts,
the other one that grows
much later, that thorn
leading up to the first kiss,
the first betrayal, the other woman
concealed behind a smokescreen
of desire. These too are dreams
about falling. He falls out of step,
falls short, falls for a woman
the way a child falls asleep
before the story ends.

He has now entered a world beyond
all his calculations. He begins
to count backwards to the first
color, the first sleep, the first
music playing. That happens earlier,
much earlier, before he learns to count
on this completely: Love ends,
stories go on untold
for years, the colors fade
into the background, vanish beneath
the body's clumsy light.

But this is not a painting
he can live with. The trees are thick
and ugly. His own face floats
out of any mirror
like the soul out on a limb,
no longer a child facing an open window
but a man having learned
the weight of dreams.

BETWEEN LANGUAGE AND DESIRE

Imagine the sound of words
landing on the page, not footsteps

along the road but the road itself,
not a voice but a hunger.

I want to live by word of mouth,
as if what I'm about to say

could become a wall around us,
not stone but the idea

of stone, the bricks
of what sustains us.

These hands are not a harvest.
There is no honest metaphor for bread.

TONIGHT I CAN ALMOST HEAR
THE SINGING

∾

There is a music to this sadness.
In a room somewhere two people dance.
I do not mean to say desire is everything.
A cup half empty is simply half a cup.
How many times have we been there and not there?
I have seen waitresses slip a night's
worth of tips into the jukebox, their eyes
saying *yes* to nothing in particular.
Desire is not the point.
Tonight your name is a small thing
falling through sadness. We wake alone
in houses of sticks, of straw, of wind.
How long have we stood at the end of the pier
watching that water going?
In the distance the lights curve along
Tampa Bay, a wishbone ready to snap
and the night riding on that half promise,
a half moon to light the whole damned sky.
This is the way things are with us.
Sometimes we love almost enough.
We say *I can do this, I can do
more than this* and faith feeds
on its own version of the facts.
In the end the heart turns on itself
like hunger to a spoon.
We make a wish in a vanishing landscape.
Sadness is one more reference point
like music in the distance.
Two people rise from a kitchen table
as if to dance. What do they know
about love?

LAST CALL

⌒⌒

I know the man who eavesdrops
at the bar means no harm,
that he washes his hands of what is said,

that if his coffee grows cold
it isn't loneliness.

I know it isn't fear that leads
a beast to water, that sleep
comes down upon the blessed,

that when a good man drinks
the child inside him begins to close his eyes.

I know when the actress lifts her glass
that the movie continues, a role
she has slipped on like a raincoat
but there's no rain,

that in an avenue of trees and
perfect lawns the world is infinite.
The doorman leaning on somebody's
Cadillac loses track of time, his eyes fixed
on the beautiful map of anywhere.

And I know in small towns all over America
the jukeboxes are rigged,
that somewhere a man takes the wrong
woman in his arms and on a dance floor
a love song falls gently to its knees.

And I know the dark begins and ends
in a place we know by heart,

that sleep runs like a river through it,
and sooner or later we are all baptized.

By now the last insomniacs
are gathering their car keys and
drifting home to their books
and the all-night religious channel

and a voice climbs down an open window
across the dark tenements of salvation softly,
across the silent tract houses,

down among the sleepwalkers; their dreaming
eyes are shut.

Juan Delgado

VISITING FATHER

I buzz through two security doors
almost unseen by the guard, busy
scanning a magazine as if he can't read.
Father waits in the recreation room.
A man slaps the back of his neck,
holding it while he rocks his head;
another sweeps the pool table's green
and smiles at me before breaking;
two women talk of paradise, of sons
too young to enter the mental ward.
Others shuffle their slippers around me,
around Father, who watches a TV and pounds
its flickering screen, saving the scene.
Noticing me, he offers the best iced tea
a quarter can pop out, but I go on,
rambling a father-talk only a son
can dish out—how quickly I bore him.
He clicks through the channels and waits
until I give up my big-man act,
but I'm too nervous to stop my chatter,
glancing at the people closing in.

"Hey, follow me," he says, waving me on.
And what a happy lady he leads me to:
Her muumuu drags on the overwaxed floor,
her mirrored orange petals shadowing her.
She sings into a hairbrush, her mike,
then giggles, raising her dress to her knees
and flopping on a chair next to us.
Excited by my staring, she spreads
her legs, digs her hand into her crotch,
working herself to half-words and kisses,

waving me closer with her dirty brush,
extending it, wanting me to sing,
but I turn, afraid to look at myself,
embarrassed and scared by her joy.
I leave Father sitting on her lap,
all embraced, walking past a screen
that jumbles voices into waving lines
and for the sake of my father and me,
I begin rehearsing what I will retell.

THE LETTERS FROM SCHOOL

Blue is for the troublemakers,
white for the award-winning students
and red for the lice-infested ones.
In spring the nurse inspects and some
lock their jaws waiting in line,
others begin to scratch and giggle
when the nurse holds the comb to light.
A few imagine they hear the "crack,"
the breaking of the louse's clear egg.

By the blackboard a stickman stands
with opened hands and a painted face,
waiting like a cross and his fingers
count the passing school hours.

A girl smudges her penciled-in heart
then folds the paper—it becomes
a bookmark swinging by her side
when the teacher calls her up.
With the bells ringing she runs,
the pinned letter rubbing her chin,
blushing through the white envelope.

At home a screen door swings,
its pumping arm brings in the night.
She translates the letter.
A hallway extends into sleep
where she sees another
locking her leg on a crossbar,
flipping, and the sand in her shoes
streams off in waves, then she stops,
raising her hand, showing her bracelet,
a tied string to ward off cooties.

The clicking of her heels
is like the calling of her name.
While she counts the empty seats,
a wooden man opens his arms.
The bookmark hides in its story.

WHEN YOU LEAVE

Carry pride in your fist,
             walk,
        stop only to check the time,
know the corner store,
                turn and smile back,
        whistling past the barking dog.

Sit at a bar stool,
        never too warm,
                never
        be the first to talk
        of politics or sports.

When listening to a lady
        never rattle
your change, unless
        she's doing you,
doing you the business first,
        Be always willing
        not to lead.

Nod even if you disagree,
                listen,
        pretending is an art.

Never repeat this,
        especially to lovers who seek
        your advice on matters.

Wear your eyes in shade,
       rest under dreamy suns,
       and sing if you have to,
       fall in love if you have to,
       but only to the day's motion,
simply silent and in transition, always.

THE PHONE BOOTH AT THE CORNER

At sixty Grandfather
stayed the whole summer.
New to America and to us,
he kept to himself at first.

After a week, he asked me
about our neighborhood bar
and so we went—that day
Mother put him under my care.
We walked by a phone booth.

The phone began to ring.
A parrot whistled from a porch.
Grandfather pushed the door.

Grandfather spoke only Spanish,
so he couldn't reply.
The door, divided by hinges,
opened by pulling a handle
but Grandfather pushed.

I leaned, trying to push.
His fear of being trapped
grew with his effort, pale
like the palms I faced.
The door folded when he gave up
and he began to laugh with me.
The bird sang and all of us
broke the air with our voices.

WINTER FRUIT

꧁

At dusk, the sun-bleached fence
shades pomegranates splitting their peel,
open to the birds,
cracking and gaping, jaws.
Some shrink in the ivy.
Moss greens their seeds.

I recall my system: First,
I put on rubber gloves
and with a wooden hammer I tap,
opening it, letting its seeds
roll and bleed on the plate.

The pomegranates ripen,
the faces of winter, the stories
of their leafless branches.
They are death's charm bracelet.

Once I sat next to them
sunning myself, letting the light
warm my closed eyes.
Their stone faces let me dream.

I saw their faces:
the bicycle boy who did not
see the car pulling out,
the housewife who was shocked
by the glaring eyes
and the policeman who aimed his flashlight
at the waiting shadow.

At night I imagine their faces
suspended on a Ferris wheel

that sweeps out the darkness
with its whirling lights.
Some figures grip the bars.
At the top lovers kiss.
Two girls throw their arms up,
screaming at the rushing ground.

TWO TIMER

True, Debby was pure as Weber Bread,
but he couldn't take homegirls anymore,
in particular La Cherry who almost sucked
his adams apple straight out of his neck
with one of those vacuum-loving kisses.
If La Cherry found out about his marsh-
mallow of love, she'd blow like a Cherry bomb;
she'd cut and watch him drip like Heinz.
Still, he was sick of that white makeup,
jet lipstick, you know, the *vampira* look.
Yet, La Cherry in moonlight would do
the nasty, holding tight all the way,
and he would stride through the school quad
with those dark hickies, rich as chocolate.

RECOMMITTED

1.

At the mental ward I chew
a button on my sleeve, looking off.
My doctor—I know what he's thinking.
I chew at the check-in counter,
rehearsing what I will say:
"Tell me again, I must give away
my rights. I want to hear why
you need for me to sign."
I walk through the security doors
knowing that later in my room,
in my sleeping ear a promise
will turn to poison, a pill
white as the button I mouth.

2.

My wife doesn't blame me
because I tell her the paint
I used at the body shop
hardened in my brains as well.

Usually, she's the first to cut
the plastic wristband labeling me
when I am released from this ward.

Behind her clothesline, she slaps
her wet hips and blames my pills
for my inability to get it up.
I sprayed cars for too long.
She doesn't turn from my body
but she holds me, guiding my face,
pressing her breasts, arching back,
asking me to fall to my knees.

3.

During our healing session,
I tap my foot and scratch my scalp.
A pill bundles all my nerves
wrapping, rolling me away.
I think of not thinking,
of working for a living,
of a yellow bulldozer
I drove as a young man.
I cleared an orange grove
of all the stumps and roots,
of all the roots worming out
of the soil like snakes.
I keep myself busy,
feeling the steering sticks
shake my hands, my body,
dulling my grip.

4.

I taste the sweat of my mouth,
crossing myself the way I was taught.
I want to rise out of this bed,
and comb my wife's hair,
smelling her shampoo.
I want to smell that odor
of a working man
and remind myself who I was.
The keepers of my sanity
bring me wax cups of water.
Outside my room they pace,
holding their writing boards,
checking me off with their pens,
but I am tired of them, tired
of the questions I must avoid,
of nods I make like a confessor.
I need only my wife,

like she is this hour,
asleep on her side of our bed.
I will curl up by her side
and listen to her breathing,
easing into her dream.

FLORA'S PLEA TO MARY

I have kissed your son's feet,
blood stained, cold as porcelain
and you bless me from your window,
a patchwork of colors warming me.
I lit a candle, watched its dance,
then prayed into my cupped hands.
Your sorrow of losing your only son
strengthens me now, so hear me.
I spilled hot water on my husband's lap.
He cursed, pulled my hair, kicking me;
I can't taste the salt of my lips.
Everything on my plate is the same.
At home my husband opens our door
as if I knocked, searching for me,
expecting me to be hiding in the yard.
I know what I must do while he waits.
When he falls asleep drunk with hate,
I will steal my children back and hide.
Until then, pain and what is not
is all the same to me—my anguish
is enough to bring you my prayers.

A MEXICAN FIRE BREATHER

Where the weather is not water
a man sips from a glass jar,
not swallowing the gasoline,
holding in his breath
while holding up his lighter.

In the cloud burst of fire
there are no legions of angels
beyond the air of his lungs,
saints holding the flame of life
on their upturned palms.

In the cloud burst of fire
the man is neither a cross,
fixed while the earth spins,
nor an ancient altar,
raised and tainted with blood.

He is only a man
cleaning your windshield
while you wait at the light.
He peers in your car,
holding in his breath and fire.

THE LAME BOY RETURNS

My smile mocked your speed—
your nicknames dragging behind.
I can't recall your name.
Has it been that long?

You bobbed and planted your crutch,
a recarved bedpost, stumping a trail.
Your other hand balanced your stride,
and waved, but I ran to my friends,
your leg a symbol of our health.
You heard our jokes and still played along,
chasing our laughter through the street,
finding me in a circle of flaring faces,
planning to run even faster from you.

Your leg did not fade
like a childhood fear,
like the creaking of my dark house.
Your limp is more than flesh,
casting a larger shadow now.

MARTÍN ESPADA

IMAGINE THE ANGELS OF BREAD

∾

This is the year that squatters evict landlords,
gazing like admirals from the rail
of the roofdeck
or levitating hands in praise
of steam in the shower;
this is the year
that shawled refugees deport judges
who stare at the floor
and their swollen feet
as files are stamped
with their destination;
this is the year that police revolvers,
stove-hot, blister the fingers
of raging cops,
and nightsticks splinter
in their palms;
this is the year
that darkskinned men
lynched a century ago
return to sip coffee quietly
with the apologizing descendants
of their executioners.

This is the year that those
who swim the border's undertow
and shiver in boxcars
are greeted with trumpets and drums
at the first railroad crossing
on the other side;
this is the year that the hands
pulling tomatoes from the vine
uproot the deed to the earth that sprouts the vine,

the hands canning tomatoes
are named in the will
that owns the bedlam of the cannery;
this is the year that the eyes
stinging from the poison that purifies toilets
awaken at last to the sight
of a rooster-loud hillside,
pilgrimage of immigrant birth;
this is the year that cockroaches
become extinct, that no doctor
finds a roach embedded
in the ear of an infant;
this is the year that the food stamps
of adolescent mothers
are auctioned like gold doubloons,
and no coin is given to buy machetes
for the next bouquet of severed heads
in coffee plantation country.

If the abolition of slave-manacles
began as a vision of hands without manacles,
then this is the year;
if the shutdown of extermination camps
began as imagination of a land
without barbed wire or the crematorium,
then this is the year;
if every rebellion begins with the idea
that conquerors on horseback
are not many-legged gods, that they too drown
if plunged in the river,
then this is the year.

So may every humiliated mouth,
teeth like desecrated headstones,
fill with the angels of bread.

COCKROACHES OF LIBERATION

for Víctor Rivera, Puerto Rico

Near the campus, every night,
there was a ceremony
familiar and savored
as *piragua*, fruit syrup on ice:
First, the student strike,
congregating on the plaza
with songs taunting
the governor and the chancellor
in rhyme, five beats of the clave,
placards accusing collaboration
with bankers and the Marines.

Then, every night,
the canter of the police,
rumbling on cobblestone
through the plaza
in the wake of dropped leaflets,
clubs sweeping at heads
like cop fantasies
of Roberto Clemente at bat,
though his spirit spat back
the water that drowned him
in shame.

Everyone had a spell for disappearing,
a secret for dissolving
between the grillwork of balconies
and fire escapes, down hallways
with a single dead bulb, basement steps.
The plaza was an empty postcard.

Later, after the flashlights
and battery-charged eyes of the cops
had dimmed,
they crept back onto the plaza,
calling to each other
with the wooden clap of the claves
and hands slapping time till
the beat bounced off cobblestone,
feasting on rebel songs
cool on the tongue
as fruit syrup and ice,
multiplying in the dark
like cockroaches of liberation
too quick for stomping boots
that circle back on the hour,
immune to the stink
of government fumigation.

THE YEAR I WAS DIAGNOSED
WITH A SACRILEGIOUS HEART

∽०∾

At twelve, I quit reciting
the Pledge of Allegiance,
could not salute the flag
in 1969, and I,
undecorated for grades or sports,
was never again anonymous in school.

A girl in homeroom
caught my delinquent hand
and pinned a salute
against my chest;
my cafeteria name was Commie,
though I too drank the milk
with presidential portraits on the carton;
but when the school assembly stood
for the flags and stiff soldiers' choreography
of the color guard,
and I stuck to my seat
like a back pocket snagged on coil,
the principal's office
quickly found my file.
A balding man in a brown suit
asked me if I understood compromise,
and we nodded in compromise,
a pair of Brooklyn wardheelers.

Next assembly, when the color guard
marched down the aisle,
stern-faced,
I stood with the rest,
then pivoted up the aisle,

the flags and me
brushing past each other
without apologies,
my unlaced sneakers
dragging out of the auditorium.

I pressed my spyglass eye
against the doors
for the Pledge:
no one saw my right hand
crumpled in a pocket
instead of spreading
across my sacrilegious heart.

Ceremony done, the flagpoles
pointed their eagle beaks at me,
and I ducked
under their drifting banner wings
back to my seat,
inoculated against staring,
my mind a room after school
where baseball cards
could be stacked by team
in a plastic locker.

CADA PUERCO TIENE SU SÁBADO

∾∾

for Ángel Guadalupe

"Cada puerco tiene su sábado,"
Guadalupe would say.
Every pig has his Saturday.

Guadalupe remembered a Saturday
in Puerto Rico, when his uncle Chungo
clanked a pipe across the skull of a shrieking pig,
wrestled the staggering blood-slick beast
before the flinching children.
Chungo set the carcass ablaze
to burn the bristles off the skin.
Guadalupe dreamt for years about
the flaming pig. Of his uncle,
he would only say:
"Cada puerco tiene su sábado."
And Chungo died, diving into the ocean,
an artery bursting in his head.

I remember a Saturday
on Long Island,
when my father dug a pit
for the pig roast,
and neighbors spoke prophecy
of dark invasion
beneath the growl of lawnmowers.
I delivered the suckling pig,
thirty pounds in my arms,
cradled in a plastic bag
with trotters protruding
and flies bouncing off the snout,

skinned by a farmer
who did not know
the crunch of *cuero.*
My father cursed the lost skin,
cursed the rain filling the pit,
cursed the oven too small for the pig,
cursed the pig he beheaded
on the kitchen counter,
cursed his friends who left
before the pig was brown.

Amid the dented beer cans
leaning back to back,
I stayed with my cursing father.
I was his accomplice;
witnesses in doorways saw me
carrying the body through the streets.
I ate the pig too,
jaw grinding thick pork
like an outfielder's tobacco.
The farmer told me
the pig's name: Ichabod.

Cada puerco tiene su sábado.

MY NATIVE COSTUME

When you come to visit,
said a teacher
from the suburban school,
don't forget to wear
your native costume.

But I'm a lawyer,
I said.
My native costume
is a pinstriped suit.

You know, the teacher said,
a Puerto Rican costume.

Like a *guayabera?*
The shirt? I said.
But it's February.

The children want to see
a native costume,
the teacher said.

So I went
to the suburban school,
embroidered *guayabera*
short sleeved shirt
over a turtleneck,
and said, Look kids,
cultural adaptation.

THE OWL AND THE LIGHTNING

∽o∽

—Brooklyn, New York

No pets in the projects,
the lease said,
and the contraband salamanders
shriveled on my pillow overnight.
I remember a Siamese cat, surefooted
I was told, who slipped from a window ledge
and became a red bundle
bulging in the arms of a janitor.

This was the law on the night
the owl was arrested.
He landed on the top floor,
through the open window
of apartment 14-E across the hall,
a solemn white bird bending the curtain rod.
In the cackling glow of the television,
his head swiveled, his eyes black.
The cops were called, and threw a horse blanket
over the owl, a bundle kicking.

Soon after, lightning jabbed the building,
hit apartment 14-E, scattering bricks from the roof
like beads from a broken necklace.
The sky blasted white, detonation of thunder.
Ten years old at the window, I knew then that God
was not the man in my mother's holy magazines,
touching fingertips to dying foreheads
with the half-smile of an athlete signing autographs.
God must be an owl, electricity
coursing through the hollow bones,
a white wing brushing the building.

DO NOT PUT DEAD MONKEYS
IN THE FREEZER

∾∾

Monkeys at the laboratory,
monkeys doing countless somersaults
in every cage on the row,
monkeys gobbling Purina Monkey Chow
or Fruit Loops with nervous greedy paws,
monkeys pressing faces
through a grille of steel,
monkeys beating the bars
and showing fang,
monkeys and pink skin
where fur once was,
monkeys with numbers and letters
on bare stomachs,
monkeys clamped and injected, monkeys.

I was a lab coat and rubber gloves
hulking between the cages.
I sprayed down the batter of monkeyshit
coating the bars, fed infant formula in a bottle
to creatures with real fingers,
tested digital thermometers greased
in their asses, and carried boxes of monkeys
to the next experiment.
We gathered the Fear Data, keeping score
as a mechanical head
with blinking red bulbs for eyes
and a siren for a voice
scared monkeys who spun in circles,
chattering instructions
from their bewildered brains.

I did not ask for explanations,
even when I saw the sign
taped to the refrigerator that read:
Do Not Put Dead Monkeys in the Freezer.
I imagined the doctor who ordered the sign,
the moment when the freezer door
swung open on that other face,
and his heart muscle chattered like a monkey.

So I understood
when a monkey leapt from the cage
and bit my thumb through the rubber glove,
leaving a dollop of blood that gleamed
like icing on a cookie.
And I understood when one day, the doctors gone,
a monkey outside the bell curve of the Fear Data
shrieked in revolt, charging
the red-eyed mechanical head
as all the lab coats cheered.

FIDEL IN OHIO

❧

The bus driver tore my ticket
and gestured at the tabloid
spread across the steering wheel.
The headline:
FIDEL CASTRO DEAD
REPLACED BY IDENTICAL DOUBLE
Below, two photographs of Fidel,
one with cigar, one without.

"The resemblance is amazing,"
the driver said,
and I agreed.

THE PRISONERS OF SAINT LAWRENCE

—*Riverview Correctional Facility, Ogdensburg, New York, 1993*

Snow astonishing their hammered faces,
the prisoners of Saint Lawrence, island men,
remember in Spanish the island places.

The Saint Lawrence River churns white into Canada, races
past barbed walls. Immigrants from a dark sea find oceanic
snow astonishing. Their hammered faces

harden in city jails and courthouses, indigent cases
telling translators, public defenders what they
remember in Spanish. The island places,

banana leaf and nervous chickens, graces
gone in this amnesia of snow, stinging cocaine
snow, astonishing their hammered faces.

There is snow in the silence of the visiting room, spaces
like snow in the paper of their poems and letters, that
remember in Spanish the island places.

So the law speaks of cocaine, grams and traces,
as the prisoners of Saint Lawrence, island men,
snow astonishing their hammered faces,
remember in Spanish the island places.

ALL THE PEOPLE
WHO ARE NOW RED TREES

~~~

When I see the red maple,
I think of a shoemaker
and a fish peddler
red as the leaves,
electrocuted by the state
of Massachusetts.

When I see the red maple,
I think of *flamboyán*'s red flower,
two poets like *flamboyán*
chained at the wrist
for visions of San Juan Bay
without Navy gunboats.

When I see the *flamboyán*,
I think of my grandmother
and her name, Catalán for red,
a war in Spain
and nameless laborers
marching with broken rifles.

When I see my grandmother
and her name, Catalán for red,
I think of union organizers
in graves without headstones,
feeding the roots
of red trees.

When I stand on a mountain,
I can see the red trees of a century,
I think red leaves are the hands

of condemned anarchists, red flowers
the eyes and mouths of poets in chains,
red wreaths in the treetops to remember,

I see them raising branches
like broken rifles, all the people
who are now red trees.

Diana García

GREEN CORN SEASON

You promised you would never keep
secrets from me. You told me
everything: how rain tinkled
on your bedroom walls; how you thought
you were dying the first time blood
spotted your panties; how your stomach
lurched when the boy you liked
asked you to the prom. All you said
that night was that you danced
in a field of green corn, dirt smell
old beneath your heels, the gibbous
moon lighting your steps as the tape
rang out *Rosamaría fue a la playa*
and you said you hoped one day
you'd swim at the beach. Now,
you're pregnant, two, almost three
months, but you haven't said
a word. A mother notes these things
about her daughter:
the way tipped breasts swell
like egg whites whipped twice
their volume, no more small whorl
of nipple brought to peak; your
unrelenting hunger for ice cream
on ripe melon, how you spoon
small bites as if to guide them
to specific cells. I bear full
responsibility. You were my grand
design, part nature-child and part
small philosopher propped in a blind
of apricot, swooning in the fruits'
perfume, a favorite book crooked

in the "v" of a branch. Often
I watched you set aside your book
to study light playing on slim,
tanned thigh, the play of skin
against leaf and bark, all part
of the same glowing world.
I watched you grow lush, tender,
pulling for the sun. Some truths
a daughter needn't tell her mother,
how we wax gibbous on beds
of disked fields, moonlight glancing
off sloped shoulders, the urge
to begin in the green corn season.

OTHER MARÍAS

⌒⌒

Once there were 50 Marías
each with 50 lovers. There was
María Luz the secretary
who crooned Latin-French-Spanish to
her Brazilian sailor, the son
of a diplomat, who brought her
music boxes from Las Vegas
where he slept with María del
Pilar who lay with the finish
carpenter who stroked her calves
as if to raise the grain on a
staircase finial. María de
los Dolores caught a lash from
the bricklayer whose dust raised welts
on her shoulders while María
Elena fixed paella for
the Spaniard who sneered at her *Yanqui*
taste for sweet beef and lettuce,
always lettuce with every meal.
María de las Rosas snuck
Marxist tracts into the copy
room for her Tijuana lover
who multiplied them hundredfold
so he could pass them to his
morenita, María la
Negra from Cuba who scored on
a *Venceremos* Brigade with
the insurance sales boyfriend of
María de Jesús (mother
of a two-year-old) who, awaiting
trial on drug smuggling charges caught
her lawyer's eye which provoked his
mother, María de los

Remedios, who refused to bless
their union saying her son who
would make a fine judge should marry
a pure María, undefiled,
not this María with child
who favored the creak and sproing of
cheap motel beds, the smoke-wine scent
of pliant sons who matched
her rising rhythm, not
this passionate María,
definitely not a virgin.

AN ORCHARD OF FIGS IN THE FALL

Somewhere deep in the San Joaquin Valley
a ranch foreman prunes limbs of fig trees
planted prior to World War I. Kadota,
honey-colored fig best eaten dried
like the Calimyrna, but smaller, tougher,
   not as sweet. Enduring.

As a child I walked light in the dried fig season
beneath the pale green glow of a hung-low
canopy, its leaves like many-thumbed hands.
Summer wind sucked at figs and dirt clods.
Bend, crawl, bend, pick, infinite insult
   to neck, waist, knees.

Any semblance of shade was destroyed
in the noonday sun. Lunch was a blur
of bean burritos, a dash to the outhouse
at the edge of the field, and a thirst
for water on a floor full of sun-baked
   rock-hard *terrones*.

Once I ran from a boy on a metal brace
who pitched and rolled as he asked me to play,
I ran from the whispered *Tuvo polio*.
I ran from an orchard of figs in the fall,
the stripped trunks and arthritic fingers,
   the grave of limbs gone wrong.

TURNS AT THE DANCE

The man who loves *rancheras* holds out his hand
gently, formally, again and again,
bends to the sound of each woman's voice.
The pattern of rejection makes him stiff.
Soy de Michoacán, he says, his plaid shirt
crisp with starch, his white straw hat tipped back,
a string tie taut around his neck. The woman
with the straight black hair looks up, looks away.
She only wants to dance, swirl the roses
painted on her skirt, forget the albacore
that scents her hair, the hours that she carved
chunk tuna from slabs stacked overhead.
This morning no one gave him work. He vaulted
to the curb each time a driver slowed
a half-ton truck or new sedan. He pushed
his way to windows, used his most convincing
English, yet the last sedan drove off
for the third day in a row. *Todo se lo
mande Dios,* he counsels, God will provide.
He wants to make her laugh as she spins
between his arms, sense a rhythmic response
when he clasps her belted waist. She feels
his callused hand catch on her back and wonders
for a moment how he'd stroke her hair,
whether it would snag. She stumbles on the beat.
As she lets him take her elbow, he ponders
could he walk her home, would she flinch
if he lightly touched her cheek? Could there come
a time when he could study how her eyes
are green with flecks of gold, watch beads of sweat
collect along her forehead; a time

when he could ask, *¿Dormiste bien? y*
¿Cómo te sientes? over morning coffee?
She steadies on her heels. She pretends
he doesn't follow when the music ends.
She weighs the invitation to the dance.

SQUARING THE NAMES

When we caught lice in third grade,
Tony's mother soaked his hair
in kerosene. His hair fell out
exposing a football-shaped skull.

    Pelón, we chanted, *Pelón,*
    cabeza de melón.

We forgot his name
but not his bald head, not
even when his hair grew back.

The Chavezes' oldest girl
wore a cheerleader's skirt
and a letter on her boxy
orange sweater.

    La Barbie, we called her,
    as in Barbie Doll, and Jorge
    was her football captain Ken.

And there was Pineapple
for his chunky shape, Shorty
because he was, and Be-tween
the youngest of the twins.
My favorites were Punkin
with her fiery-red hair
and Hollywood for his gold chains.

For a while I was the *barrio*
sweetheart, *la consentida,*
with my Shirley Temple curls
to my waist. Too bad I wore bifocals.

Bookworm, brain,
Coke-bottle eyes.

My aunts switched to Spanish
when I came around. I stayed
bilingual. When they caught me
listening to the gossip about
my godmother, her boyfriend
ten years younger, they shrieked:

¡Coliche! ¿Quién te invitó?

I told an uncle that he lacked
the right chromosome
which was why he only had
daughters. I'd read that somewhere.

I'll never forget how my mother
signaled with her eyes,
warning, yet amused,
how my uncle hollered,

¡Cabrona! Somebody should wash
your mouth out with soap.

All these names I saved for myself.
When my mother introduced me
to her uncle last year, she said:

Soy Tomasa, esposa de Manuel,
y ésta es mi hija, Diana,
la más grande.

There it was, the formal genealogy:

"I am Tomasa, wife of Manuel,
and this is my daughter, Diana,
the oldest."

I am Diana *la cazadora,*
keening calls to the hunt on moon-hard nights.
I respond to *orejona,*
ears bent to the shape of your sighs.
Call me *la chismosa,*
your secrets glide in neon past my gaze.
Summon me with *cabrona,*
rutting female goat,
name of admiration
for those who won't back down.
Beware *la hocicona,*
the unmuzzled jaw,
the one whose heart rules her tongue,
blaze of tongue flaming strife.

LA CURANDERA

She shuffles to the door on faded scuffs.
Her breasts sway beneath the bodice of her muumuu
and the hands that welcome me are warm,
the skin like old paper crumpled then smoothed.
She is *la curandera*, faith healer, my *nana*.
We face each other, child to grandmother,
the trusting balance of young to old.
"*Mija*, did you give it to the priest?"
"did he bless it?" she asks. She takes the emblem
of the brown-skinned Virgin from my palm.
The sun is in her face, her eyes water.
Some say she can read minds. She makes us drink
infusions of *gordo lobo*, fat wolf,
when we are sick with fever from the flu.
She prescribes a tea of *estrella de anis*
to calm the itching rash of measles; a tea
of *manzanilla* for those who can't sleep.
The new Irish priest didn't understand.
"Witchcraft," he snorted, and refused to bless
the scapular. So at Mass I placed the badge
with its rubbed-smooth image in my prayer book
hoping to catch stray blessings. *Kyrie eleison.*
Tonight the old women of the neighborhood
begin a *novena*, nine days of prayer
for a dying man. Dona Juanita attends,
her black lace shawl clipped to her bun.
Her husband lies on their bed at home, swaddled
with sheets fresh from the line. The women fan
their black damask skirts on red Windsor chairs.
Nana displays the scapular. Hail Marys rise.
I can never go to heaven if the old man dies.

SERPENTINE VOICES

～∞～

1.

How many voices can I plum in this poem? Tricky poem sometimes in the first person "I," sometimes the "we" plural, not imperial, because voices collect as in sometimes the story is mine, as in me, the author, the first-person narrator, but sometimes we are all voice, girlfriend, *mi amiga, de parte de,* on behalf of all my girlfriends from long ago.

2.

Fresno slumps late summer.
Raisin grapes dry on brown
paper trays. Crepe myrtle,
purple plum burnish the campus,
student body twice the size
of my hometown. Winemaking meets
a general ed requirement, finals
served at the Gallo winery.
Agriculture majors milk cows
at dawn, saunter back to plates
of thick bacon, butter-basted eggs.
Some become lawyers; others
yearn for family farms,
or better, agribusiness concerns.
I never knew their names.
But their faces, sun-thick
and neckish, grimace
from across the barricades
as we chant *¡Huelga, Huelga, Huelga!*

3.

Khaki, everywhere khaki.
Not us, boy.
Our dads wear khaki

in the fields, khaki
cruddy with suck plums and peaches,
khaki topped with white
dress shirts pressed
by mouthy daughters
who iron their hair
so it drapes over breasts.
Daughters who swear
to wear miniskirts
and tight, tight dresses
when we're outta sight.
We'll be so outta sight.

4.

Laura's so goofy over him,
his Emiliano Zapata moustache
and burning eyes, the raven waves
of his hair. All he needs is a horse,
a hat and he could be the poster
boy for the movement.
Campus Crusader.
Campus Crusader at the microphone
crooning fight songs to the masses
severe body taut beneath poncho
and requisite khakis.
Exquisite.
¡Qué tonta!
As if he cares.

Campus Crusader took lunch
with the college president.
They scrutinized the weather
("Will the rain hold?
Do raisins mold in the rain?").
Then Campus Crusader promised
we'd vacate the library.
He may have promised names.

Somebody should tell Laura
his wife in Sanger fled Durango
when she was 17. She packs tomatoes,
packs his parents to the doctor, packs
their son to day-care. She sends him
care packages when he's too broke to eat.
Somebody should tell Laura
about the WASP girlfriend who keeps
an apartment in his complex, a real
wasp, you know, wasp-thin waist
in a hive of drones. If this weren't
1968 I would call her anorexic.

5.

(This voice of mine keeps interjecting, intersecting. A voice, not that
choking *silencio*, not that pestilent marshland of a *vacío*. Because we were
something, God, we were something else.)

6.

As if short skirts make a bad
reputation. *Nalgas,* heck yes,
you can see my *nalgas,*
full curves beneath a white summer dress,
the only way I'll ever wear white again.
You who always liked my ass,
who swore you'd always take care
of me. You with your preacher talk,
so respectful to my parents, *¿Mande Ud.?*
whenever they asked you a question.
I never would have opened my door to you,
never would have slipped beneath the sheets
so scared you wouldn't like me enough,
scared you'd tire of a nervous virgin.
If I'd known you'd go back to her. . . .
What reputation do I have now?
I may as well give it to everybody.
Lárgate de aquí. I never want

to see you again, you and her,
and you tell me she's pregnant.

7.

Rosie/I got pregnant. Her/my
lover swore it wasn't his/their
fault. It was *cinco de mayo/*
16 de septiembre
and we/she/I/he/they broke loose.
Loose hips whipping through *cumbias*
ankling through *rancheras,* hips
grinding through night-long sets
of lovemaking, the intensity
of a rolling tent revival. Rosie/I
had a miscarriage/baby. Rosie/I
thought I/she was lucky.

8.

He never told anyone he couldn't swim. I didn't know he couldn't
swim. He didn't have to swim. We "tripped." My Yoko Ono to his
Dylan Thomas. We'd play "Knights in White Satin" at dawn, steam
brown rice, sauté onions.

I loved his body. He had one of those small-muscled bodies. Each
knot and ripple etched his skin, bronzed like our daughter's first shoes.
He called me lush, his hands sweeping long, slow, then Morse coding
closer to the goal.

Our goal. He would publish his first book of poems by 25; I'd teach
math at a local college. I reached my goal.

I didn't go to the lake. Instead I see every night, behind my eyelids,
water toying with his chin, his lips, his eyelashes. No one notices. No
one hears his shouts, "I'm drowning, I can't swim," this big joke, this
grown man who never left the fields long enough to find a pool and
learn to swim.

My husband knew how to live. He deserved to live.

¿Que viva la raza?
Yes, I live,
he did live,
we shall have lived.

9.

We weren't unaware stuck here in this deathbowl of a valley. There
were just more pressing matters. We knew about the moratorium. We
had brothers in Vietnam. We knew the death count Dan Rather never
talked about. Just give him a live feed and let him sail away. Hey, he/
we didn't want to know the truth.

Remember the hunger hearings? We were there. Taking shorthand in
English and in Spanish and then transcribing our notes all night. We
fought for food stamps instead of those god-awful commodities, wee-
vils in the macaroni and rice, beans so dry that a week's soak wouldn't
get them back to plump.

10.

Hey, *ese,* you heard about that righteous
lawyer down south, a real *carnal,* man. You know,
he got the people off who marched on that church
on the white side of town. Man, he's got so many *rucas*
he can't even keep track of them. *Pura madre!*
He's got a book out, you know, calls himself
a bull or something like that. Yeah, and he
wants to write a book about *el movimiento,*
something about *cucarachas.*

11.

I hate cockroaches. Fuck that metaphor! You don't have to tell me
how it works, I know how to read. Those sick little mothers survive a
nuclear explosion and come back stronger than ever. The implication is
you can step on us a million times but we come back in droves. I've
tossed out my share of roach motels. I know where they end. Better a

roach at the end of a roach clip any day. Anyway, cockroaches come apart in the city. All that stress. Out here in the country, anything can thrive—roaches, people, raisin grapes. Burnt brown and juicy, enough folds and wrinkles to offer surprises for the rest of anyone's life. A treat. Sweet, iron-rich, sustaining.

12. Coda

Levántate, no pidas más perdón. . . .
A dry hot wind *zings*
through my pores.
I ponder the fate
of betrayed loves,
extinct buffalo.
Chilled beef tongue
cradles in crystal,
delicate flavor enhanced
by fresh garlic,
tomatillos. I created this dish
for myself.
You never made it for me,
you couldn't
make it for yourself.
I listen to Los Lobos
by myself, pour a tall Pepsi
(free ad space here)
for myself.
I will live longer than you.
So the actuarial
tables say. And at the end,
I'll be better off
tongue married to a sauce
simmered long after buffaloes
disappeared from the plains.

TÍSICA

No one calls me that here. No one
ridicules my sallow skin, the bags
beneath my eyes, the racking coughs
that jerk my torso as if twined to
a puppet's strings. No one whispers
behind my back that this is God's
retribution for a sinful life. Instead
here in the Ahwahnee Sanitarium beneath
Yosemite's Half Dome, we are all consumed
by cough and sweat. At daybreak, veiled
nuns collect ochered sheets. I approve.
Removed from friends and family, allowed
no close contacts, we bask invisible
in a rarefied air of pine and wealth,
numbed isolation in nature's preserve.
We flatten clay, form rows of Half Dome
ash trays, spoon holders, coded messages
urging release. If air alone could rise, sift,
dissipate strains of tuberculosis passed
among families confined to migrant camps,
I should have fled this sanitarium
months ago. Instead, I stall with rows
of patients labeled unclean, unclean, *tísica*,
nightmare of the poor, the dread disease.

THE CLOG OF HER BODY

Breathe in and out, legs in stirrups, bottom up, eyes focused on a faded happy face tacked to the ceiling. Next to it a smiling Burt Reynolds asks, "Did you check your breasts today?" Each time the doctor presses, you grit, grin, clutch the nurse's hand.

You had a hard, big body like the mahogany bowfront that held your family's china. Your boyfriend said he liked your legs—a fawn's legs tapering to small, graceful ankles, the rhythm of your heartbeat on your instep. Your mother warned, "Keep your panties on, *mija*, I won't be responsible if you take your panties off."

That first time you got pregnant, stretch marks silvered from your crotch to your *ombligo*, shone with lotion that you rubbed until your panties looked like parchment. For Easter mass, you squeezed into a blue and white striped minidress and slipped into your red leather heels.

When you left church that day, a middle-aged man in a gray Oldsmobile—fins snaking down the street—pulled alongside as you walked home and offered you a ride. It was Charlie Cruz, Nadine's dad, the one who looked so sexy at your high school graduation.

Remember how he looked you over like a box of nuts and chews: your belly out to there; your copper-penny face; hair pulled back with a tortoise-shell barrette. You said, "No, thank you," and he asked, "Well, what if we just took a little ride somewhere?"

And you said, "*Muy agradable*, Mr. Cruz. I could use a bathroom. By the way, excuse me while I pass some gas. I don't get morning sickness, just this gas."

You could have called his wife, said how you saw Charlie down on Sixth today, how fine he looked in his best silk tie and asked could she stop giving him liverwurst for lunch.

When you had your daughter, there was the boss who pressed himself against you in the copy room, peach-scented hair, mint mouthwash, white flakes dusting his pink forehead and rounded cheeks. Andy was a brilliant man, four degrees and no profession, a supervisor at the welfare intake office.

When he accidentally touched your milk-hard breasts, mentioned how they were the largest sweat glands on the human body, you thought of how he'd look if you offered him a peek, unsnapped your shirt, removed the now-soaked, yellowed nursing pad that reeked of sweetly soured cream.

When you got home, Ronnie rubbed the spot in the middle of your back, the ridges on your shoulders where your bra straps dug too tight. Those were the nights your breasts leaked if you slept on your side or on your back, never mind your stomach.

And when Ronnie ran his hand up your thigh, kneaded for a while the softest part, then moved his way along the folds, you cried, "No, my stitches." He wished that you had murmured, *"Ven acá, mijo,* what a fine big boy you are."

So when your doctor says it's all worn out and you need a hysterectomy, listen to his hum as he spreads you wide. Hear him compliment the thick moist walls, the way your juices run so clear. Feel his rising heat, the lust for meat, when he repeats his offer. And when he clips you with his speculum, don't be shy. Stick your cervix out to there before you spur him in his sides.

A MATTER OF CONTROL

∽∾∽

Don't be afraid
at night
on the street,
in the daytime
on the beach,
only one other
keeping time
on the beach
with you,
on the street
behind you,
then silence.
When you turn, he
is almost on you
calf leather slip-ons
step-for-step
with you, so quiet
on their toes. Don't
be afraid
to run, to hide
inside your eyes.
Keep yourself hard
as he stumbles.
Brush your shoulder,
breasts, hips, when he
runs past, runs on
to the next corner,
over a dune, down
to the next wave.
Don't be afraid
when the phone
rings late at night
and a voice smooths

your floral tights
around your ass.
Perhaps it is
the neighbor's son:
listen to his voice
crack when you
say his name.
Heed the whisper
on the wind
when you are alone
and the moon is full
on the desert.
Study the lines
of the Joshua tree
taut against the sand.
Wear a dress made
of hemp, earrings edged
with feathers.
Invoke the names
of the grandmothers.
Hear their council
in the humming rock.
Cry the *pee-ik*
of the nighthawk
mouth wide,
head thrust forward,
your shadow long
against the land.

RICHARD GARCÍA

THE BOOK OF DREAMS

∽

If you dream of scissors,
two women, one light, one dark,
are whispering your name.

If you sit on the front stairs
at the bottom of the sea,
you are going to spend your life
waiting for someone.

If you are on your knees in the closet,
digging through a pile of shoes
you are going to learn something
you do not want to know.

"*Madre, dime,* what if I dream of the moon?"

"The moon is a woman, *Hijo,*
she comes, she goes,
she changes her mind.
She has power over women.
This will give her power over you."

The book of *One Thousand and One Dreams Explained*
is the only book in our house, and every word is true.
It's big, so big you have to climb a chair
and use both hands to lift the cover—

both hands turn the pages
that stretch out like wings.

∾

Being old is not so bad. You wake up
from a nap and it's a new day in a new world,
at least, that's what I say when I wake
to find myself in a rocking chair on the front porch
of the Swannanoa Convalescent Home.
What do I see when I look out at the sun
going flat in the haze of the Smoky Mountains?
I see chickens, thousands of them marching two by two
into the sizzling glow, as if into a frying pan.

Back in my carnival days I used to hypnotize chickens.
I'd hold one close to my face and stare straight into its eyes
and that chicken would freeze and plop over, stiff
as an old boot. Waving my arms, the cape, mumbo jumbo,
that was just showmanship. Who would pay to see a man
staring at a chicken? Obstinate. That's their whole problem.

Chickens are obstinate just like apes who could talk
if they wanted to—if they wanted to, chickens could fly.
I don't mean jump from a barn or into a tree but fly,
fill the sky, migrate, rise with the vultures on a warm
spiral staircase of air. You could put them in a wind tunnel,
maybe just a big, clear plastic tube with a fan at one end,
pull up and down on strings attached to their wings,
and play some stirring music like John Philip Sousa
or the theme from *Rocky* and they still wouldn't get it.

Dreams I had, words I might have said, something I read,
they get mixed up until I can't tell which was which.
Did I really catch Richard Nixon in my hen house?
And did he say he thought it was a voting booth? Was there
a gunfight? And did I leave town hanging from a rail,

tar and feathers my only clothing? I seem to remember
throwing an entire chicken dinner at the ceiling, my wife crying.

They used to love my act, I'd look down from the back of a truck
at all the blank faces, cross-eyed, beak-nosed farmers,
a drum would roll and I'd put that chicken's entire head
into my mouth and bite it off. The crowd would scream.
I'd spit the head into some lady's lap—flap my elbows,
knock my knees together, strut, crow, cock-a-doodle-do,
and spin that chicken over my head, sprayin' blood like rain.

DANGEROUS HATS

Trying on a hat in the shop
I suddenly became much taller.
I looked down at my wife
and smiled with one eyebrow raised,
like a pirate inspecting
the latest batch of hostages.

I put another hat on and I was
leaning back in a chair on a front porch
with my foot on the railing, a snake-skin
cowboy boot sliding out of my jeans.
Squinting into the heat lightning
that lit up the horizon, chewing on a toothpick,
I thought of you old friend, and I wondered,

would I ever see you again, would you stride
toward me taking shape in the haze,
and what hat would be tilted rakishly
on your head? Not the captain's cap
from your sailing days
or the ten-gallon from Montana.
Not that creamy confection you won
from a millionaire in Nepal.
Not the black cap you stole
from a drunk SWAT cop
in a trucker's bar in West Texas.
Not the feathered explosion
you traded for a shrunken head in Borneo
or the hat that survived
the machete attack in the Mexican desert.

No, if I should see you again
you'll be wearing some hat I can't imagine now.
Some hat you could throw into the air
to sail away over treetops and return,
suddenly appearing at your feet days later.
Some hat still smoking, smelling of danger,
a hat snatched off the head
of the devil himself while he lay sleeping
by his private trout stream in the underworld.

ELITE SYNCOPATIONS

Glancing at the wicker
nightstand I had just brought
for her, my mother
was not surprised, after all,
wasn't this the same
nightstand she had in her room
in Mexico
when she was a child sixty years ago?
And when I happened
to play Scott Joplin's "Elite
Syncopations"
on the phonograph she smiled.
Back in Mexico she was a child again
on her way to school—
she had been told to hurry
past the cantinas—
but she and her girlfriends
loved to dance
to the music that poured out of the swinging
doors, the ragtime
waltz, the cakewalk, sparkling
with a touch of sadness.
I'm not surprised that I have the memory
of running across
a courtyard with my mother while bullets
pinged and spattered off
the walls. "Stay down," she told me,
as we pressed our faces
into dust in an alley and she threw her black *rebozo*
over my head.
"And whichever side wins, wave and yell
'*Viva!*' when they
ride into town." Now we are on a bus trip

that we never took
deep into the interior. Second class, nights
of no sleep,
our sweat odorless, as if we took baths
from the inside out.
It's a battle of raised and slammed windows,
of lose your seat
if you get up, of hold your pee,
wooden slats pressed into our bones,
and ignore the man
masturbating under his jacket. The three nice nuns
who sit in the back
have something to show me,
a fetus one of them
keeps in a small jar of formaldehyde.
"*Viejito*,"
they call him, wise old
man with wrinkled brow,
little blue man sleeping. The hills
loom up darker
than the night and my mother says we are passing
her hometown.
"What's it called?" I ask. "It has
no name," she says,
"and the people there are bad, gangsters,
all of them."
The little man who knows everything
seems to agree,
with just the hint of a smile, floating, tilting
this way and that,
he lies low, his dreams always level to the earth.

LOS AMANTES

I play marimba on your rib cage
while you whistle through my thighbone.
We click clack up down escalators.
You rattle around me
taking tiny elegant steps,
whisking your skirt from side to side
as if to fan the flames
my feet stamp out.
We rub our pelvises together,
shilly-shally through lingerie
locking our bones in a romantic puzzle,
my teeth clenched to your ankle,
your hips around my neck.
Who can say this was a man
and this was a woman?
My bones love your bones.
And when I am rich enough to buy skin for you,
I will stretch it over your bones
like paper over a kite.
What a pair we will make,
strolling the avenue in the evening—
me in top hat and tails.
You with your skeleton of blue fox
slung carelessly over one shoulder.

A DIVER FOR THE NYPD
TALKS TO HIS GIRLFRIEND

ꚃ

I can't even see my hands in front of my face
through the darkness   mud, raw sewage,
black clouds of who knows what,
gas and oil leaking out of all the cars
that have been shoved into the river.
But my hands have learned to see,
sliding sideways down wrinkled concrete,
over slime coated rocks, broken glass, plastic bags,
barbed wire, as if there was a tiny eye
at the end of each finger. There are sponges down there
shaped like puffed-up lips, with silky tentacles
that retract at my touch. For some reason, all the grocery carts
in the city are making their way to the bottom of the river.
Did I tell you about the body wrapped in plastic
and chains, and the pile of pistols, rifles,
enough to start a gun shop? Once, looking for a missing
Piper Cub, we found it next to a trainer
from World War Two, both parked side by side
as if waiting for permission to take off.
People throw strange things in the river,
I don't know, some kind of voodoo—jars
filled with pig eyes, chickens with their throats slit
stuffed into burlap sacks. Everything—TVs, couches,
lamps, phone books—is down there—if we ever grow gills
and live in the river we'll have whatever we need.
Today it was a fishing boat missing for five days.
Easy to find now by a certain odor that seeps
through our wet suits, that we call corpse soup.
The fishermen were sitting in the cabin, bloated hands
drifting as if they were swapping stories.
We tied them together and rose toward the surface
in a slow spiral. Once, I was feeling around in the dark

for this drowned lady, I was about to go back,
to call it a day, when her arms shot up
and grabbed me tight, tight around my waist.
Even when we're out of the river there's more water.
Bath, shower, bath, shower, disinfectant, rinse—
but I never feel clean. Everything seems dirty: crowds
in the market, car horns, alarms, the barking of dogs.

BRIEF ENTANGLEMENTS

∽○∽

Two dogs stuck together. The male lifts one leg
then the other over the bitch's back.
Still stuck, they face opposite directions.
As each tries to run, they spin, all eight legs
a circular blur, into the path of a speeding car.
Just as it's about to hit they break apart.

The car is driven by a couple
late to their own wedding
who were trapped in a traffic jam
where they sat without speaking,
occasionally slapping each other
like puppets in a play.

I'm on the bike path, my ten-speed
meshed with a young woman's mountain bike,
my hand on her bare thigh. I cried out
when her handlebars locked into mine
as she was trying to pass. She remains
silent, calm, as we fly along
like insects tangled in midair.
She wrestles us apart and speeds ahead.

I slow to a wobbly stop. The dogs run off in opposite directions.
The bride and groom will acquire a certain fame
for their skill at holding one kiss
as they drift through a car wash like divers sharing air.
I am leaning on one foot, almost tipped over.
The young woman rides high on the pedals
as she speeds away. Turning her head back
over her shoulder she calls out, "Sorry!"
I am sorry too. My palm tingles with an afterimage—
something smooth, muscular, yet incredibly soft.

EL ZAPATO

Not the wooden spoon,
primordial source
of sweetness and pain,
flying at me from across the kitchen—
I barely bothered to duck.
Not my father reaching for his belt,
I would be long gone before
it could slap across the table-top
in a sample *nalgada,*
but my mother's shoe, El Zapato:
black leather, high-topped
with the long tongue laced
all the way up, thick square high heel.
Shoe from a hundred years ago,
puritanical shoe, witch's shoe,
shoe of the Dutch Cleanser lady,
peasant shoe, gypsy shoe, shoe
for clogging around a hat flung down
on the grave of your enemy.
Not the pain, brief humiliating clunk
of leather striking flesh,
but her aim, the way I knew that
if I ran out the kitchen door
down the back stairs, over the fence,
around the corner, if I glanced
over my shoulder while my arms and legs
were flailing away, El Zapato
would still be there, its primitive
but infallible radar honed in on my back.
Even now, years later, El Zapato
sails toward me turning slowly
like charred meat on a spit.

It lands on the bed with a thump,
and clamps on to my foot. I kick
the blankets, as if my foot were stuck
in the mouth of a dog,
an old dog, without teeth.

NOTE FOLDED THIRTEEN WAYS

When you speak to me I feel my blood sliding
beneath my skin, and I remember my father.
I see him behind your eyes, as if I stared
into the past through the wrong end of a telescope.
He used to take me to cowboy bars and pass me off
as his girlfriend. I remember Old Spice aftershave,
Hank Williams's "I'm So Lonesome I Could Die," the two
of us slowly turning to that sad, ghostly waltz,
his smiling down at me, the envious glances of strangers.
Later, walking along a tree-lined street in the dark,
I would hold on to his left arm and let my right breast
brush against it with every other step
in a kind of marching rhythm. I wanted him all to myself.
Is that why I once snipped off my sister's braid while she slept?
Why, when he went away, I would take his letters to Mother
from the mailbox and hide them under my mattress?
He used to call me his Little Femme Fatale, his Lady in Red.
"What I like best about you," he'd say to me,
"is that you're like me, capable of betrayal."
I used to fantasize we were sidekicks driving
across the country robbing banks in small towns,
that I would walk into a jail where he was being held,
me all innocent in a gingham dress, Mary-Jane shoes,
white stockings, pull a pistol out of a picnic basket
and set him free. I wrote *I always desire my teachers,*
on a scrap of paper and slipped it into your notebook.
You will never know who wrote it. Even if you took me
in your arms you would not know because I would disappear,
lifted, completely taken up, enclosed into something large,
warm and feathery. I would be a country road that stretches
into the distance. You would be a dark cloud arched
over a white horizon, ragged at the edges, raining
streaks of black rain that never touch the ground.

THE STORY OF KEYS

If you would give me
the key to your house
I would think of it
as a one-dimensional
mountain range.
I would hold it up
to the sky
and study how clouds
drink in its valleys.
Think of it
as a tiny file
that cuts through
vertical shadows.
The door of your house
would be a rectangle of light

that shuts behind me
trapping the moon
by the coattails.
I would no longer need
the twisted path
that brought me to you.
It would disappear
along with the forest
that popped up
on springs and hinges.
And the stagehands
and roadies of my dreams
could put away their props—
cups, pools, musical perfumes
darker than your hair.

Entering for the first time
would be as if I never left.
And I would tell you
the story of keys.
They were made long before
the invention of doors.
Although no one knew their function,
wise men suspected their importance.
Carefully, they would place them
into the cracks of tree bark and twist.

Anything can be a key: a piece of wire,
a safety pin, laughter.

RAY GONZÁLEZ

BROWN POT

And so I eat from a brown pot,
sticking my fingers
into the stomach of the seed,
smearing them with laughter
and the growling voice.
I eat from a brown eye,
its carving pupil leaving my sight
to enter ladders of fingers,
the mistaken belly of a scowling fool.
And so I eat from a brown hand,
opening my leaves to fill the room—
odors, smells, gases from the juice
my father left when he fried
a goat and called it god.

I eat from a brown pot,
its greasy sides glistening with words
I first learned when I was full—
anguish, hope, stand up and spit
the extra stem from the woven heart.
I swallow the chasing worm,
mutation of protein and the tired tooth,
making me taste the lines of demolition—
digested truth escaping in the wind
no man calls his own without a name.
And so I sit and belch and need,
wishing the picked bone was the tool
used in tracing lines on my face,
the way the cook cut her hands
and fed the pot to make it brown.

I eat from a forgotten brain—
scooping thoughts out of the skull,
licking the bone to see again,
listening for the hum of the tongued ear.
I eat from my first body,
asking for crumbs to come alive
and change hunger into
the shape of smoked-out rooms
where women chanted and cooked
fear into a *masa* to shape the man,
take him into the world for years.
And so I eat from a brown pot
on the greasy table, fill myself
with the chewing of voices,
shards of clay sticking in my throat,
deepest swallowing before stuffing myself
with the livers of what is fed to me.

CABATO

Cabato—the art of tying sticks together with brown twine to make a secret symbol only the maker knows.

I tie eight sticks together,
make sure they look like
the first star that fell at my feet.
The brown twine is tight,
finished, wound around
the middle of the long,
smooth bamboo sticks.

It is not a star.
It is a falling diamond
that used to be the closest pyramid
that rose near San Luis Potosí
where my grandmother was born.

I make my *cabato.*
It has sixteen points resembling
the cage of sorrows.
It is two feet long
at its widest point,
a twisted wreath for those
who want me to tell them
what it means.

I twirl my *cabato*
in my hands.
It is a bamboo forest eliminated
when the first people
found my grandmother
and gave her the will to live,

allowed members of her family
they didn't kill to flee.

I hang my *cabato* on the wall.
It looks like a flat reprieve
in what I always wanted to create.
The sticks will remain.
The mutated star and points
will dry into the wall
until the day I die.

I touch my *cabato*.
No one knows what I think
when I make sure
the twine is secure,
the geometrical cross
I have made a part
of the same weapon
invented by the first man
who tied anything together.

THERE

There is the voice of confinement in the pine cone,
a surge of prism, cups of laughter
hiding toward one shoulder, mistaking the naked back
for the need to run and demand everything stop.
There is the chamber of falling into the coiled hunt,
speaking so fast you will not be remembered
as the green chameleon that hides on the back porch,
swelling his throat into the crimson bubble
that belonged to the eclipse.

There is the ritual of courting the mud
and the onion that won't grow,
a hummingbird becoming text,
beating the bee to the pollen that wasted years
getting to the mumbling spore, a tiny circus
caught in your throat when you discovered
there was no way in, no water coming up
from your sweat, the error of holding down
the temperature of the earth.
There is the shape of the stomach,
the horse drawn upon the neck,
a red scratch from the white and pink roses grown west,
fungus on their brown leaves carried in your mind,
reference to any rose a pulse you thought had no name.

There is the manner of becoming two men,
one for the asking and one for the wish
of holding on to the wicked son who abandoned
your home to dance with his real father,
grabbed by the boys to run wild in the streets,
leaving you to wonder what tongue had gotten in,
which language had glowed, the words you overlooked

in the graffiti that took days to wash, the signs of no return.
There is the fire big enough for childhood,
the toys you miss—a captured box of dry weeds,
an empty carton of milk, a small wooden ball so light
you toss it in the air each time you call
your third-grade friends to come back.

There is the beetle glistening in the pueblo,
spelling no with its black wings,
its green and silver bands removing your memory
of its crawl up your arm the night you lay in the dirt
and told a story in order for them to let you up,
recount how you grew two heads on your shoulders—
one for love, one for fleeing the flooded river,
the path of every beetle that swarms and buzzes,
sounds tied to your ears by string you cut off a kite,
wound it around one leg of the *chicharra* as you rose
from your rocking chair, an old man eating the wings
of flying things landing in the bowl set before his broken legs.

THE ANGELS OF JUÁREZ, MEXICO

Sometimes, they save people from drowning in the river,
their wings soaked in the oily water
keeping them from leaving the border.
The oldest angel is a man from the last century
whose white hair hangs to the ground.
He floats above the water each time he saves
a *mojado* who tries to cross in the *coyote's* raft,
falling into the current to be somebody.

The angels of Juárez look over the *colonias,*
nibble on the cardboard shacks like the rats
they never fear because rats have their own angels.
When children fall into the poison,
the angels dance above the glowing waves,
pull out the chosen child with a kiss,
toss him on the bank for others to find.

The angels know about revolution and dying,
prefer to hover over the Río Grande
where the bodies move at night,
fighting for air angels mistake
for a grasp toward heaven.

The angels of Juárez often hide
from the desire to cross,
to take a chance and send a chant
over the dirty waters of the border,
the latest drowning victim wondering
why the old man he was told
to watch for, never extended a hand.

The angels appear in the night,
listen as the course of the border

tightens with searchlights
and the hidden green cars of patrol.
They swim over the electricity,
wings humming to create a magnet
that makes it easier to cross.

The angels never appear near the churches,
nor the kneeling altars.
They are not part of the prayer, the escape.
They know the river churns toward
the horizon that accepts fewer souls each year.

They hover to make sure
the water keeps flowing,
mud moving to the other side of the river
where no angels dwell because
this side was cleared of faith long ago,
waiting streets of El Paso
never mistaken for the place of angels.

STILL LIFE WITH ENDINGS

✦

For the cracked dish
with the dragon branded on it.
For the glazed finger
in a sculpture of a winged woman
slipping her mouth around the cock of a man
who has never known the power of stone.
For the man who gives her his life
as the rectangular landscape where it matters.
For the wheel of the mountain
ending in an earthquake no one felt.

For the mango sucked
before having to confess
how many shadows
landed on the island.
For the voice interpreting
a new language to children
wanting to write their first poems.
For husband and wife staying together
through the pain and the joy
of distance, closeness, love with
the growing vegetables in the shrubbery.

For the music written
when there was only one child to sing it.
For the artist who left this mark
that will never be deciphered.
For the fish hiding under the lily ponds
until darkness brings them out
in time for the diving osprey.
For pebbled ceilings following
the closeness of a family

who built the house, only to leave
when there was a misunderstanding.
For high windows that reflect
the rain that has no reason to fall.

For Mexican riddles and ghosts
from the sanctuary rising
to change the direction
of the boy fleeing his country.
For an act of contrition
and the way a list of forgiveness
lies without shadow
in the corners of every image.
For the last elegy of a mother
wanting to be burned
so her children can forgive her.
For men visiting their dead fathers
in the kitchen of a stranger's house.

For collecting dried pine needles,
trying to glue a design out of them
onto a polished piece of red wood.
For waiting to be given
another time and place,
a uniform of colored maples
that swing in a wind
too powerful for the cottonwood.
For the hope of asking a loved one
to select a mask from the closet.
For the crime of having
too many shirts that don't fit.
For the selection of souls
thrashing outside the door.
For the last meeting with a mentor
when no questions were asked.

For the time I was helpless
and had to take down my vision,
close my eyes and pretend
I was someone else who did not
worry about losing my hands
in the stream of water
that poured out of the cliff
when I finally reached it
after climbing for two days,
discovering this was the place
where I was tied down by the invaders,
strapped to this table of rock,
pierced by holy vowels
that cut into my wrists.

BEYOND HAVING

And, always, there is desire
like the orange and banana changing texture
on the kitchen shelf.
Their skins heaving slowly into themselves.
There is the liquid of lust and thirst,
an open gloss of choice and cutting,
a lying down toward the wind,
the heaving you were warned about.

And, soon, there is love
like miniature spellings embedded in the shoulder,
waiting to be misspelled, washed,
brought back by the shadow of perception that fades
with what moves below the arm,
hinges on the doubt cried away.
There is the mistake of giving name to the prune
and the print bitten off and covered over
by black hair whose numbers are kept secret,
whose long strands belong in the tale of the carpet,
the pomegranate, the hundred ways of staying there.

And, besides, there is the danger of riding desire
until it carves you into its swollen throat,
steel-cry of possession and the infinite blessing
of fingers missing from the first time,
fingernails tracing the shape of the strawberry
to memorize roughness without leaving.
There is the flavor and the understanding,
a place to rest the eye after much traveling,
one force for what binds you together
without you knowing red marks on your backs
are places where wings would have risen
if you were angels.

WITHOUT VILLAGES

The June heat exiles our real needs.
Streets melt in hundred-degree heat.
The enormous pot of *menudo* boils on the stove.
In the Lopez bakery, *bonillos* are only nineteen cents.
Four cinnamon cookies for thirty cents.
The baker comes out of the back drenched in sweat.

Someone is going to collect a knife today.
The motorcycle cop knocks on the wrong door.
The homeless vato drops dead,
only to wake up as a fox terrier in another life.
No one knows about this.
My uncle told me about him.
He didn't know his name.
He loved the dog.
It got hit by a car, but the vato
never came back after that.

Even here, in another room,
the brain hums in the night.
It is like a pickled pig's foot
embracing the old cuento of the fat *Mocoso*
breaking into the restaurant late at night,
breaking all the dishes as he ate
the leftover *chicharrones,*
the *tripas,* the cold rice that was pounded
into the trash bags to be set out in the morning.
Mocoso even ate two huge bags of *tostadas.*
The police never found him.
They ate in the restaurant one morning
and knew why he broke in.

Let's repeat the song of
the mysterious center where the beautiful girl decides
she is going to save the world
by taking off her clothes for a dirty old guy
who is a friend of her father's.
They do it at his house and she is surprised
how much she liked it.

She is surprised her father finds out.
She is surprised he shoots the guy.
She is not surprised her father does four years.

By the time he gets out, she is a single mother
with three kids, on welfare, a bruised cheek,
and has not seen their father in several months.

She is still beautiful after all this
because the song of the mysterious center
has something to do with the father who did time
and the mother who kept silent all these years,
helpless to do anything about her daughter.

Unknown fountains.
The drum wrapped around the head of a fish.

Coughing tigers lying down to die.
The priest begging the Lord not to teach him more prayers.

Smashed acoustic guitars mounted inside a volcano.
Early tickets to the bus ride.

Late moves down the mountain where a tribe vanished
never to be discovered or dug up by anthropologists.

The hero waiting for the plane to land.
Unmated sources of disease eating the human body.

Four billion wild cells cavorting on the tip of the nose.
The watercolor artist dipping her brushes in milk.

Running doves landing in water.
An odd three-inch orange and green bug with

transparent wings that look like antique combs
brushing the hair of a happy woman.

An attempt to skip each and every vowel
and get to the message beside the glass of water.

A tired man organizing a festival.
Electric wires through the heart of an ape who knows there is a
God.
Fears that the truth contains the whole story.
Courage to dismantle the bread rolls and pass them

out among the rich, the wealthy, the ones who
would devour them without saying a word.

Marriage as the giving and guessing of what
the other desires when there is time to believe

every breath we lock away for each other
is every year we will outlive those who don't care.

Invocations and the redeemers gunned down.
A fat city full of crime, fires,

smoke, broken glass, mistaken identities,
neon signs, sirens, paved roads.

A fresh bowl of very hot green chile sauce branding
the lips of a sweating young boy who went into the place

because someone was following him,
someone was going to teach him about the seed.

AT THE RIO GRANDE
NEAR THE END OF THE CENTURY

∽

See how the cottonwood bends at the waist.
    It turns grayer, cracking as the sun goes down.
There is no limit to returning.
    See the trunk turn toward what has changed you.

When you place yourself against the river you can't reach,
    it is an old habit draining your hands of strength.
Look at the cottonwood disappearing.
    Its hidden sediment is alighting out of your reach.

It is not water.
    It was not made to mark the border with leaves.
Only the river can cease its mud and turn its brown heart.
    Only the passage belongs to swollen, bare feet.

What you know is the scent of the desert you are so tired
    of writing about,
how it covers the past and hangs as the ember of thought—
    wisdom molded out of the falling world.

What you love is removed from the pale circle of shadows.
    It will never return. It will weep.
Even the moisture in the armpit smells like the trees.
    Tomorrow you will see another kind of growth.

See the threads of the hills turning back the revolt.
    See how the men are crossing the river toward you.
When the cottonwood petrifies in the lone spot,
    history will be overlooked and you will die.

What you keep are the thousand miles of the wounded breast.
    What you smell is the fine cotton of the dying tree.
When the white balls stick to your hair, listen to the fleeing men.
    Even their backs are wet and some of them look like you.

SAVIOR

I look into the eyes of loved women.
I kneel and pray each week.
The difficult bird flutters out of my navel.

I'm going somewhere else.
I'm going somewhere drumming.
I don't know if it is spoken about—

When the bird leaves, I become a man with two legs.
When I run, I am loved.
When I stop, the sculpted fish on my wall borrow my spine

because I'm going somewhere to be handled
by icy trees, streets that cry, and nights
that come to me in three languages.

CALLING THE WHITE DONKEY

I called the white donkey who hurt my left shoulder
the last time it appeared next to me,
ramming me with its ivory head, cracking my back
to relieve me of worry and hope.
I called the white donkey,
surprised at the sound of my voice.
I was scared, wondering if the white head
would reach to give me its donkey brain,
snowy matter dripping into my ears
like the horse of the first man who fell off,
the fire in the mind of the donkey teaching me
about white desire, the white moan, white hair
on the back of my head that warns me.

I called the white donkey.
It came slowly toward me,
huge ears shaking with growing fury,
the smell of its breath turning the air white,
a greed wanting to bite into the white apple
I have carried in my throat since I was a boy.
I stood and faced the white donkey, watched its
slow gait become a shuffle of possession,
shaking its head as it stopped
to root its dirty hoofs in the ground.

I stepped back and clicked my fingers.
It would not come closer, its snort commanding
I listen as it farted.
I walked away and did not know it was I
who had yearned for labor of the ass
which comes so close before letting me know
the white animal I summon can't remove
the white scar from my heart,
white streak of a blind life I live for good.

MAURICE KILWEIN GUEVARA

A RHYME FOR HALLOWEEN

Tonight I light the candles of my eyes in the lee
And swing down this branch full of red leaves.
Yellow moon, skull and spine of the hare,
Arrow me to town on the neck of the air.

I hear the undertaker make love in the heather;
The candy maker, poor fellow, is under the weather.
Skunk, moose, raccoon, they go to the doors in threes
With a torch in their hands or pleas: "O, please . . ."

Baruch Spinoza and the butcher are drunk:
One is the tail and one is the trunk
Of a beast who dances in circles for beer
And doesn't think twice to learn how to steer.

Our clock is blind, our clock is dumb.
Its hands are broken, its fingers numb.
No time for the martyr of our fair town
Who wasn't a witch because she could drown.

Now the dogs of the cemetery are starting to bark
At the vision of her, bobbing up through the dark.
When she opens her mouth to gasp for air,
A moth flies out and lands in her hair.

The apples are thumping, winter is coming.
The lips of the pumpkin soon will be humming.
By the caw of the crow on the first of the year,
Something will die, something appear.

THE MINIATURIST

✦

I make tiny, tiny huts,
the hills, too, are tiny,
small hills, small trees,
a silver river, a forge with smoke,
and a little blue water tower.

To work on such a minute scale,
I use magnifying lenses,
jeweler's goggles,
sometimes even the instruments of microsurgery.

Perhaps you have seen some of my pieces?
The Sun of Copernicus. The Ferris Wheel.
The Funeral Parlor (how difficult it was to glue the greenbottle fly
onto the right index finger of the corpse). Or
the one for which I am famous: *The Lovers of Late Afternoon.*
Her hair falling back, the red at the tip of his ear,
the universe of heated molecules, just above their bodies.

THE MAGIC CARPET

∽

What you need to know
happened two weeks before
the little creature
(with three teeth missing)
found his grandfather
splayed out on an Oriental rug.
The rug was a gift from long ago,
the family's only possession.

A fortnight earlier
a national burial tax
went into effect,
legislated from the mountainous
and faraway capital of Bogotá.
The tax was the brainchild
of a young senator from Tunja:
So many *pesos* per corpse,
per interment,
would be extracted
like golden teeth
from each grieving family.

But the little creature,
his mother and his father
could not afford the indignity
of the new tax. So
that Wednesday morning
before breakfast
they wrapped the *abuelo*
in the Oriental rug,
and the father carefully
loaded the grandfather

and a shovel
onto the bed of the old truck.
The plan was to drive
deep into the hills
and make a private ceremony.

But the little boy grew hungry.
And the father grew hungry.
And the mother needed food also.
So they stopped somewhere
for twenty minutes
to eat. When they returned,
the mother began to cry:
¿Dónde está? ¿Dónde está Papá?
The Oriental rug was gone and instantly
the father prayed to San Cristóbal
as the mute child studied the shovel
pointing east.

THE EASTER REVOLT
PAINTED ON A TABLESPOON

∽∾∽

¿Dónde está el pueblo?
El pueblo ¿dónde está?
El pueblo está en las calles
buscando unidad.
Los pueblos unidos
jamás serán vencidos.
—POPULAR CHANT

Above everything, I make a jagged, blue edge
and the Andes. Along the front and back of the handle,
I detail a greenhouse of fourteen thousand roses.
From the scooped tip as the tin rises, I place the President
of my country on the balcony of Hortua Hospital. Shouting
into an already antique microphone. Ordering the army
on horseback to charge. To destroy the squatters' camp.
Hear the constant thudding, the long screams,
the galloping over mud. How it sounds
when the boy with five hundred roses
strapped to his back raises a burning branch
to touch the horse's chest. To show that motion: hooves
and the olive uniform falling through the mist. To freeze
the instant of boiling water splashed in the face
of a young corporal. I steady my hands to focus:
the quick slice of a bayonet through tarpaper, rocks in flight,
the revolvers popping until you can hear nothing buzz,
the hundred bodies of Policarpa filling up a common grave
in the pit of the tin spoon. I paint the basilica on fire,
as a wild, orange dove flies out of the stained glass.
On the back of the belled end, I make the other world:
where my mother lifts a clean shirt out of the aqueduct;
where my father shepherds our only cow, without a stick,
up the mountain from the grassy suburbs below.

MAKE-UP

∽∾∽

This before Trotsky and Breton
before the murals of Diego Rivera
the intrusion of September 17
or the dream of wind and papaya

    Green Coyoacán
in the bedroom mirror
Closing the left eyelid
Frida paints Orizaba
slowly
an ash triangle
rising up to the black brow
and a little moon
with a monkey's face
in the violet sky

Opening then on the dresser a Spanish fan
and fanning like a bird's wing till the coolness dries

    she closes the other eye
    and from memory makes up
    a curving landscape of dark seeds
    shiny inside the fruit
    and the ghostly curl of one new life

    It is afternoon
Like a sleepwalker she moves to lie on the bed
Wind is blowing through an open window
This is before the little deer and the portraits
It involves the prophecy being carried to the gallery
It is the revolution of one girl dreaming

THE BUDDY HOLLY POEM

It's so easy
when you realize
that all the squirrels
on the shingled rooftops
of Milwaukee
are Buddha
that all trees shake green
in the wind
that the moon is you

Sing
that the whole of every note
is individual and one
that love is free
every day
on the blue earth

Listen to me

THE LONG WOMAN BATHING

Although he can not admit it even to himself,
these are the years whose possibility he has always dreaded.

The man in the room listens to cars and rain, unfolds
maps that have failed him, lines tracing absence along the dark
    interstate.

If a friend were to call him on the telephone,
the man would drawl, "It's like I'm being stalked in a dream."

In the gray light of the television it happens that he awakens
on the floor and studies his overcoat hanging, remembering the old
    self.

He is twenty again and running in the museum from room to white
    room
where he finds her in the Bonnard, the long woman bathing in the
    lilac water.

And were it possible at any moment he might cry out:
I refuse her ghost, I refuse to dart like a deer in the open.

TUESDAY SHAMAN

Say it is Tuesday
that he sits beside the road,
slowly chewing a shaft of snapdragons,
the red liquid rolling down his throat.
He flicks his magic tongue to read the air:
one is falling in love,
one is coming to him with a question,
one is dreaming of warm bread,
one is combing her mother's hair in the city
when a stray bullet enters her soft skull
(then the dark child sleeps forever)—
everything he tastes is written on the wind.

I have thought about it.
Now I'm not sure.
It may be some other day (not Tuesday)
that he sings death in three languages,
in the English language,
in the Spanish language,
in the Chibcha tongue of dreams,
belching a perfumed breath,
volcanoes in his palm,
counting the infinities,
rolling cut cornflowers through his hair,
mourning once again the four crazy loves
that left him sitting beside the road.

ABUELO, ANSWERS AND QUESTIONS

∽∾∾

I.

Abuelo, why are there flies?
They're reporters for the dead, mi joven bestia.
What do they report?
If the millonarios *won or lost.*

2.

Abuelo?
What?
I forgot.

3.

Abuelo, who puts the scorpion in my bed when I'm asleep?
Why, is there one when you wake?
Yes.
Dead?
Yes.
Don't worry. The dead don't sting.

4.

Abuelo?
What?
How old am I?
Almost five years old.
How old are you?
Old as bones. When the moon was born,
I was already eight years old. . . .
When I was a boy, I lived on the coast of Colombia
and rode the fins of blue whales at night
from Barranquilla to Nantucket Island
and back, this before dawn.

5.

Abuelo, why do I have steel hooves?
To kick truth in the ass.
Abuelo, why do I have shiny hooves?
To dance a little cumbia. To play with mirrors.
Abuelo, why do I have hooves?
Because they run in the family.

LONG DISTANCE

~o~

(two Sundays before Lucilita's coma)

Pennsylvania to the coast of Ecuador, my mother calling her aunt,
the nurse picking up, relaying the phone, and the woman
under the sheet says nothing. This morning I saw Walt Whitman
half-buried in the blowing snow of the foothills. This was two
   weeks ago:
my mother saying in Spanish to the silent woman *We miss you*
We love you We think of you every day and waiting
the four thousand miles. Delay. *Lucilita.* Saying nothing.
Until finally, my mother asks *¿Me oyes?* Do you hear me?
Te oigo: the only words the old woman says. I hear you.
Singing under the snow. Singing under the falling snow.

Juan Felipe Herrera

THE POETRY OF AMERICA

∽∽

Of the sixty-two
viceroys who served in New Spain, three of them
had private Indian mistresses and fourteen of them had mulatto
children.
They flayed skin and drank oyster juice.

They burnt corn tribute to Huitzilopochtli
in the name of Yahweh. I raise my arms to them.

Salut, I say. Salut. In the center of the table.
I can see their nakedness; this harpoon, I carry, in their accent.
This invention of being.

I must dive deep to find my father now.
In this office there is little to save except the disintegration
that plagues all species. I have learned to play the piano
and the clarinet. This is my new awareness.

I wear a bluish wig. I have learned to kneel
on water, outside where the old women loosen their clothes.
Ocelotl swishes his knife blade. He shows us his teeth.
The Central Valley coughs and fumbles for words.

How to describe this illusion:
in New York, the Metros have rusted on their tracks.
Another homicide tells of this. Chiapas lives on bagels and tequila.
They know the history. They know where to find the President's
children.
They read Artaud in Braille and rub their genitalia.

A sandwich, a Cézanne to mix things up a bit. Bologna or
ham on rye, garlic butter. More. Duck sauce and raspberry sausages.
Lobster, *ostrón* and *calabaza*. We must eat.

We must crash through our faces
and discover the new opening.

Eat the gold,
chew the strings, digest until we are ribbons,
reddish and jade green. Chinese and Vietnamese.
Cambodian and Hmong villages in tuxedos. Manila
and Northern Luzon where the Ilongot seek the words
for the new revolution.

FUTURE MARTYR OF SUPERSONIC WAVES

∽◦∾

Kerouac &
an American President's wife fuck in frenzy.
Spill the vodka and scream in Polish.
Quote Polanski and Rozewicz. Hide the cut ear
and the swollen lips. Erase the tooth marks on the buttocks. Erase
with Titanium White and Thalo Red.

Kerouac is old. Rescue him in Venice Beach. Buffalo meat, organic
    carrots
and Coltrane. Chuchifritos and Quaaludes. Congas and acid.
All I can see is an elastic frame.

I am in bed next to ten people who I don't know. One of the
    women stretches
her arm for another hit. The needle jams and splits through her.
    Les McCann
drools in the smoke and pumps another hit to cool the pain.

I rise burning,
my head, a clump of patchouli. Slump towards Santa Monica. Like
    Zappa in
Ben Davis black. Like Guthrie in trench coat, leaning forwards with
    a woman-
shaped shadow slung across the back.

There I go. I go singing, Godadavida. Hula dancer and spit drinker.
Smoke waste and waste deep. When the world begins I will be
    there.
I tell myself. Do it again. Do it with Yaqui knowledge, sip on the
    bubble
inside the heart. Inside the plasma. Listen
to the tracks, how they blow sparks in the night and churn the
    names

of the ancestors, how they rub on the cocklight, the brown-black
Sutra hole trailing over Tijuana where Don Colosio kissed the light.

Wear this jacket,
wear it for me and we'll go arm in arm, breasts out,
for once, plucking air, drops of anise & milk. My boots
slide down to the Silver Dollar where St. Salazar was drilled,
where St. Salazar was hauled, in a Mexican gurney, where
we sang to him in Jewish phrases, where we gave him oxygen
and Mexican flesh worship.

RESURRECTION OF THE FLESH

The gold triangle is my enemy.
It speaks with Chaucer's heart,
it rattles on about the English penchant for redemption, about
the necessity for virgins in the time of holocaust. It calls me in a
    fake
Pakistani accent, so I can take up my woman's vest
and call my sisters.

I am coming from the left side,
in my mother's white gauze, in my aunt's last handful of nickels.
A circle of women climb above the mountain; Frida's again,
Gertrude's and Georgia's.

The hand of a man wants to follow but he cannot. The Macehuales
and the new Viceroy have sent the cadaver of Cortez back to
    Mexico City.
In Seville, they grieve him, in Catalonia all is quiet, all is sacred.

I am in love with Hera.
I am reading the glyphs on her belly,

tarnished coins with the face of Socrates. My thighs are muscular.
Her skirt is shredded by my heat, by this ablution I make every
    Sunday
morning. It is time to begin the inquisition, they are saying.

Behind me. The men are crawling and speaking in broken Aztec.
They are saying the mulattos will win this war. They are afraid
that the new God at the center will speak and stand on his mutton
    legs.

I raise my cup and toast to Georgia. I raise my shadows. I walk
on bone stilts to the mound where they are dancing. The earth
is conical today. Angles and labia. Woven calf muscles. My head

going down. I can see that my womb is split and a red jacket
reaches into me. Out of me.

Batwing. Testicles.
Ovaries and cymbals in ash-colored clouds.
Hide my face.

Take my eyes for nipples and suck me.
I want to carry this chair of hives and dancers. I want to solve
these Spanish numbers. A brown blue, a gold fleshiness.
Only the bust in the cave remains peaceful.

THE YELLOW ROOM

~∞~

                                        The table gleams
the easel contains an ochre/liquid/you'll return to that table/you'll
    finish
that picture of sketches gray/you'll lift yellow dabbing it on canvas
her forehead her beauty marks on her throat her hair her slender
    arms resting
on an easy chair her ankles her knee the oil fern buried in the
    infinite
stone of her eyes the mantle of water covering your back embraces
    your neck
bites back breath wants your saliva take her earrings and unravel
    them
on the paintbrush although you didn't think you knew my name
    when you
asked me how old I was yes you knew but it doesn't matter I've
    always
known you since the days when you listened to barking in the night
walking in circles outside a house full of Protestants chanting with
    drums
when you took me to the eucalyptus trunks and forced me to touch
    the folds
of the broken branches ringed with the heads of ants we counted
    them and
you laughed because I had never seen them before you kept looking
    at my neck
you said that it too was a trail marker toward the dark and then do
    you remember?
we ran between the parked cars near the theaters and bent the
    antennas/in the
hospital I found you lying down and you told me about the
    beautiful child of
your womb about its tiny hands and its voice near my pillow but
    you never

got to see it in fourteen years you only saw it the day it battled the
    heat of
us seen together at the table with him in this world/the snakes
    devouring
the silhouette of your brothers when they buried your father/they
    didn't take off
their jackets because they had to travel three days to the funeral
they had to see you and the small woman who wasn't their mother
    the strange one
the tiny one your mother sweeping up the wax and the bitter smoke
    swirling
over the grass and you shouted at me/Jaune you'll trace the petals
her eyelashes after a long time you'll trace the dark bird sleeping
upon her hands with the ink from your fingers you'll close the
    curtain
you'll open a crude cupboard getting out a coffee cup and counting
    the automobiles
out your window for an instant you kiss a child/
in the air.

The table gleams.
A stain. A droplet. A watery amarelha/yellow. Buzzing/the voice
    inside the boards.
That stain calls/lamb/walks down the hallway/the movie theaters/
    seeking
exit clawing the mat it breaks lamps of liquor and blood and
stumbles over rings of rags and hands of asphalt asylum and
nightjackets full of naked men women praying at the moviescreen
pins and fruit on paper legs the movie of 80 years of insomnia with
    eyes
all tied up velvet tongue that unties and loses itself in the dark box
    of laughter
carpet and patent leather heels and rolls to the front of the cameras
    and
touches steel and turns to purple prêta cell light the lips tremble
    cordero
lamb dies/loving a shred of film the immense sheet of foam sorrow
    covers

the whole window/he/sees/examines that cup of black eye in the
   center of his hands
and drinks with his pupils the reef the tresses that float in the room
   and
takes a step and caresses the table/lifting the paintbrush with fluid/
   branco
white you erase the door the branco/white padlocks crossing the
   room
in the restaurant you saw her on the linoleum after four five six
   years
you saw her you finally saw her sleepwalking watching you for a few
   seconds
radiant on a sunday stroll buying packages chatting with the man
   who was she?
were the scarlet shoes new? whose blouse with triangles? the lips
   they kissed
you cold distant extended transverse layers filaments lines weak
   reddish the slow
dry air oval ebony bouquet of voices a thousand voices of dust and
   nights and furies
the water on the waistlines boiling the hoarse naked skin her womb
   cymbal
of shredded seagull waves on the cliffs the salt knot burning the
   thighs
the crazy drizzle of whimpers branco corderos/white lambs in/the
   corner
of the bed. They're looking for the invisible door/

The table gleams. It is time?
to confess the transparent old people/the pious priest prostitutes/
the hunchbacks with their rosaries of sores their crucified feet biting
the concrete below your pulpit/never!/reaching the deformed
   foreheads
riddled full of holes by your smile forever beating the table
   overcoming the ink
nothing will be yours/your hands will be unable to smooth on
chainlinks/
your handsome slaves love you/still

your insects which carry immense statues of bread without vulvas
    without
nipples without testicles without howls of earth moss sperm/
come close/sweating/she/wants something from you/is she mute?
alone?/only her hands burn gold/come closer/she wants to touch
    you
but

It's only a picture/monochrome/Jaune the dead body circling
    watching your
cage

WHEN HE BELIEVED HIMSELF
TO BE A YOUNG GIRL
LIFTING THE SKIN OF THE WATER

Hold up the right corner of the sea,
pleated. Lift it and find pleasure snoring, cut open
by crystal and stone.

Look down at your shadow
by the sands, by the gilded whiteness of your legs.

Below you:
a wrapped hydrogen scarf, an ink cactus stuck to the dry galaxy
below the sky veils. Touch down. Come to the ground, the talc,
this desert—peeled and washed by distant clouds.

My hair reddish, down to my jaws. When will I blow
the conch shell? Shall I awaken the sleeper below?
Who is he following with eyes closed?

The perfume is solar. My nakedness is simplistic.
As the sleeper searches, I find America rising on his back,
mottled, brownish. Above the water, the stone folds,
clutches itself, peeks through holes and rivets.

We are playing.
All of us, then just one.

The sand has been swept with a wide brush. The girl—
pensive as she lifts the folds of the water. One hand.
One arm and on the other the conch shell waits. Poised.

I know the stone is the secret.
The secret in the shut mouth.
When I was five I cut my fingers. I cut off my thumb.

I delivered ice on the back. Wolves sang from the mountains.
Julian, the violin man next to us,
in the Mexican village paced his floor.

Julian knew his wife, Jesus, was shaking
and another man was raising her hair.

PORTRAIT OF WOMAN
IN LONG BLACK DRESS / AURELIA

That morning you took the wind
in your hands
I didn't think it was possible
to slip one's fingernails in the joints
of space

You took the gray sidewalks
all alone like rumors
because your feet didn't care
to construct destiny's
precise formulas

And the tree
its trunk of blood among the flowers
you took it like a man
burgundy sack black lips
you said it was your husband
and
the sea what was it?
was it your son?
was it your thousand-handed son scribbling
your name over the sand?
was it your father
running voiceless in a streak of smoke
toward your shoulders?

That morning
between your hands
the sun and three birds
were searching for you in the stars

THE DREAM OF CHRISTOPHER COLUMBUS

⌒

They carried her above us. As we walked
over the new lands engraved with conch shells and spears
tagged with red and violet flags. The ship
was at the center of things. In night sweats and shattered shelters.
   No longer
in the village. The new cross bled as my son walked forward. As he
   lifted
his knee and sang to himself.

She was above me. The transverse cross
and archbishops lined to my right. Naked in the waters.
The women had been taken away. This is the frontispiece
that is etched on the new treaty.

In Phoenix they speak of this to the children. New Orleans
and the gumbo in the pool halls. Jazz, wicker chairs and gout.
All the signs tell of this.

Now we have ice in the heavens. Cities of water quartz and shorn
   sails,
whipped lungs of ice and enigma, a large belly of fences to soothe
the new parliament. The boys are handsome and yet they grow sad.

What will happen to Mexico crashing against the United States?
This is on the frontispiece. This is the spirit that invades under our
   shirts.
I take her down.

It isn't enough that we see her body looking up?
The bluish halo isn't enough? She lies there curled and frozen,
yet her face breathes in.

I take her down with my thick hands, with my short breath.
Swish my hair across my shoulders and ask her about the ship
   behind us,
my son's gait across the flat lands, into the basin, into the fauna.

The dirt softens with each new step. I am concerned with space,
with the uncertain ghosts stalking the territories.

~~

in memory of Ramón Medina Silva

In August he boarded the bus/the A.D.O./for southern Mexico and
    saw
the hunched posts/those gray tree posts/one Emiliano Zapata
one woman with contraband rifles/orphans in uniforms of fury
against the sugarcane growers of Anenecuilco/stopping time and its
    veins
the year 1914 coughed in the splinters/behind the rocks his horse
in green mourning was scratching the dust of commanders/in
    Iguala/the moon full
of huipiles of blood and rust/bitten cartridges/you saw him in the
    darkness of
throatless generals/their torn muslin undershirts purple with the
    rage
of lizards/but you didn't want to talk to him/I knew you were an
    old woman
with small dark hands/he knew you would never come back to see
    me/you never
wanted troops/you wanted something on your breasts/some torn-
    out light/for your house
for your children an eternal seed in the joints/of those withered
gardens you pointed toward Morelos/that highway/where Lucio
    Cabañas denounced
the soldiers' grins/with centuries of fever in the eyes that gave you
life/so alone/why?/what are you doing on this barren land?/the bus
    is full of sand
the suitcases drowning in ants/the soldiers brought us some papers
and told us that in Mexico there was hope they made us/cross
    ourselves
they ordered us into a single file/toward a gold hotel full of
architects in robes designing/the wallet of stars and/you followed us

I wanted to touch you/your shoulders were whispering/you took
    me to your mountain
house/of missions and tin slums and you open your hands and I
    look into
the abyss/the smoke/the president's rattler
and the infinite flame in the bones of your/
children

CHERRY BOWL WITH BLUE REVOLVER
Neo-American Landscape

࿓

A cherry bowl with a blue revolver
for a heart.

This is America:

a spider web on 10th Street
where my father began to die;

my half-brothers and half-sisters stood
so far above me and didn't say shit;

a synthesis of camouflaged faces
after a voluptuous murder;

the phantoms
of Central American mass burials
descending over Mexico City
in the form of an earthquake;

seventeen-year-old prostitutes
putting a few slugs in their weakling lovers;

the apple merchant asking the dark widow what's
at the movies? Maybe, a good show, eh?

A promising executive in the Palace of War
whispers, *what is Beauty?*

And, they respond:

This beggar's bowl at your feet, my son.
It will follow you wherever you go.

ATAVISTIC: TRACES AFTER THE RAIN

My hand is up. It goes up to my father's dark coat,
he turns and raises me further up to him.

We walk along the center where the sheets of the earth curl at will,
where the migrant rocks shift with the wind.

The landscape and the characters have been washed away
by an unknown surf. The choir sings in the background.
Foreign languages and motifs. Wagnerian, flattened
with Dufy's dirty brush.

There is more sky than usual. A hole drills into the scene. An egg
    without
songs or reminiscence, a flurry of memoria, restored and mutilated
    by many
years of wandering. This is at my short shoes.

This is in my father's wilted pockets.
He is dead and yet he speaks and pulls me
towards his favorite Texan city. He loved there, he says.
He met my mother there, in the dance hall
with two accordion players.

My back resembles a cape, a cassock,
an insect silk, a fender shaped and cared for by the driver.
I live here on occasion. I live in a boiled sky; I entertain
sand shapes, rivers and ripped land. This was my calling.
This was my craft for many years.

I walked with my father's taciturn manner. I skipped through his
    open desert
and taught myself the languages of midday. I spoke in cloud fevers,

I leaned against the stones that carried my inner structures, my wet
    soul
flickered in the quarry. When I passed by, I touched the flecked
    edge
and kissed every striation. This was all I had.

My father named me. He spoke of Acapulco,
Cuernavaca and mentioned Sarajevo only once.
He cried when he spoke of her. She had raised him

with goat milk. Sarajevo found him on the road—
favored him as a baby. We walk gently.

Hold up the bone shank,
this femur shard that makes it possible.
Step toward the sculpted cities of Civola.

DIONISIO D. MARTÍNEZ

THE CULTIVATION OF ORCHIDS

This boy with the eyes of an owl
will not grow wings.
Instead, a man who lives on air will grow
inside him. In time, many arms
will sprout from the boy's
body, which knows how to adapt
from one life to the next. When the man
grows too large for the space he occupies

and the boy starts to ache and complain,
the man will learn to twist one foot, bend
his knees just so, relax the neck
until his head comes down and rests
between the shoulders.
With the man correctly positioned, the boy

can lie down, his skin draped tightly
over his rib cage, and we will not notice
this other life inside him.
He will need all his arms to carry
himself, to keep the two lives from coming
in contact with one another.
In time, the boy will outgrow the man.
His arms, having become unobtrusive

and ordinary, will welcome
the sleeves of heavy coats.
His eyes will look progressively smaller.
The man will give himself a voice
and a name. The boy will begin to hold
his breath and eavesdrop
on conversations between the man
and the woman who has come
to draw him out.

A DISCREET PRAYER

❧

They said the war was over.
They made the dead children sing.
The children had no voice:
death has no voice. They said the war
was over, and they blew out the roof
of the great cathedral, and they
called out to the sky. Ana was very
drunk, but she remembers. She
was wearing her dark glasses
and her idea of American clothes.
The war was over and Ana had no voice.
She asked me with her hands to speak
for her. She begged me to say
that the children were dead and the dead
have no voice. We danced in the street
in front of the great cathedral.
Ana kept falling like death itself,
falling on me, falling on the street.
I could've fallen in love on that street.
The walls of the great cathedral would've
given me their blessing. Ana
would've dreamed daylight through her glasses.
She would've stopped dancing and falling
and begging me to speak for her.
The dead children would've called out to the sky.
Instead, we kept dancing. Ana kept falling.
The walls of the great cathedral
were voiceless, like death. I composed
endless letters home to America,
or my idea of America.

Father,
what do you do with a girl
who has mastered the art of falling?

Endless letters, elaborate lies.

Mother,
I've fallen for a girl who goes
blind when she dances.

Their replies were little more
than weather reports from a distant country.
I spoke for Ana, for the children,
for the terrorists who prayed
in the ruins of the great cathedral.
Then I lost my voice, and deserted
the street and the girl.
I came home with nothing but the music.
They say the war returns occasionally,
like American clothes and old movies.

KINESCOPE

❦

Johnny Guitar is watching Duncan Renaldo.
Roy Orbison
is growing out of Elvis like a new
limb or that extra syllable every other
word acquires in the South.

What happens when you run into yourself?
You burrow deeper
and deeper until the center
is all there is, until going further
defeats the purpose of going.

You quiver inside yourself, your hands
gripping the spine, your eyes amazed
at the thin frame that sustains everything.
This is your own center of gravity.
This is the man you have become.

My father watches Duncan Renaldo. Duncan
Renaldo watches the moon in the sound studio.
He thinks the sky owes him a living. As if
living were something we did outside the body.
My father knows better.

We know what happens when two mirrors
face each other. I want to know
what happens when they stand back to back.
What kind of annihilation,
what self-devouring hunger for nothing.

MATISSE: BLUE NUDE, 1952

⌇∾⌇

I fail to cut your hands
in proportion to your head,
your bowed head in proportion
to your breasts, your
breasts in proportion to one
another though only
the left one is visible from
this angle.
Where did I put the missing
hand, the eyes,
the small blue
breath of what you will say
when you see yourself naked
and begin
to speak to the unrecognizable
blue of your form? You will wait
for an answer from what
you think is a stranger.
Why do I talk about strangers
when I should be talking about
the recalcitrance of my hands,
how my fingers
curl up and refuse to follow
the images I have in mind for them?
I keep seeing the two strangers,
nothing but the sound of blue
in what they call breaking the ice:
one speaks, the other pretends
to listen. I cut a blue
path into your heart because love
is more manageable than paper.

THE DEATH OF ISADORA DUNCAN

There must be one thing that makes you shiver—
small rain, November, a handful of lies, renting
a room where the river wounds the city.
Whatever it takes. Crossing the river, renaming
the bridges. Whatever it takes
to shiver like the rest of us. We held
fast to our hats and turned up our collars
when the wind rose from the dirty water.
This side of the river, though, we made
the mistake of thinking we were safe.
We didn't see the Arab who followed us for miles.
We didn't see the car with a mad driver,
the lights out, the radio blasting foreign
propaganda. We didn't hear the radio.
This side of the river the theaters were showing
Coup de Coeur. More foreign propaganda,
they said. More neon. More illusions. Let
them live on illusions, you said.
But not even the trumpet player in the movie
could make you shiver. You walked out
cool as a note that fades into the hum of traffic.
The next day we went to the cemetery to count
the famous dead. I was sure you'd shiver then.
But the thought of knowing that fame
offers no guarantees didn't do the trick.
We stopped at the grave of Isadora Duncan. Then,
walking back to the gate, we found a simple grave,
nothing special except for the tree growing
out of it. We didn't know if it was a bad joke
or a plea for eternity. It was November,
dusk, the first clear sky in days.
We watched the sun holding on to the branches
of that tree, holding on for life. We watched

the branches burn and turn to frozen ash.
You pointed out the lack of grace in the death
of Isadora Duncan. On the contrary, I said.
There was the race car and its handsome
Italian driver, Isadora beside him, her shawl
trailing over the side of the convertible
and catching in the spokes of a wheel. You
thought she died like a character in a bad joke.
I saw a flawless choreography: it wasn't so much
the instant of the strangulation as the series
of accidents leading up to it that killed Isadora.
A shawl, you said, looping your own shawl
once more around your neck. You shivered
like fading sunlight, like a branch about to fall.

STANDARD TIME: NOVENA FOR
MY FATHER

∾∾∾

We're turning back the clocks tonight
to live an hour longer.
I suppose this is a useless ritual to you now.

Late October brings life to the wind chimes
with that perpetually nocturnal music
so reminiscent of you.

I memorize a small song, a seasonable dirge
for the night that lives outside my
window. I call each note by name:
All Hallows Eve; All Saints Day; all the souls
in my music pacing, talking to themselves.

All day I sit by a statue of Saint
Francis of Assisi, birds on his shoulders,
nothing but faith in his hands.

At dusk I return to the house you knew
and a life you would probably understand.
There are night birds waiting to
breathe music back into the wind chimes when
the forecast calls for stillness.

I still remember what you said about belief,
how you laughed when I said I thought
the world could carry the cross I'd carved
around my shoulder and through my fist.
The world is busy with its clocks and its
wind chimes and the night birds that never fly
home once they learn the secret of exile.

I let out one sigh that is almost musical.
I know you can hear this much.
I take a small step back and picture
you here before I light the last candle.

All the souls in hell couldn't set this world
on fire. Even if they prove that our lives
are mathematically impossible, we
will cling to the last flame in the equation.

NOCLURNES

I.

He closed the deal on the night. A real
bargain, he said. And the city was reduced
to a room, the man's constant body in bed,
the sheets glowing like phosphorus.
One flaw in the design made it possible
for an occasional body to slip in.
The sheets would glow a bit more brightly
in its presence. Each time it left, the body
would leave more of itself behind,
until there was no absence to speak of.
The man began to count on the occasional body
and its lingering presence, which he now calls
memory. He understands that the laws
of necessity draw their own conclusions.

2.

Even night is a product of residual light.
What they call absolute darkness is the art
of knowing how to lower the shades almost
completely, knowing exactly how much is enough.
We measure the varying degrees of shadow
in the residue. We know that a shadow
is the object from which it is cast.
We are beginning to understand the principle.
Night, we have finally admitted,
cannot extend beyond the things it evokes.
The concept of night as entity is impossible.
The varying degrees of light in each shadow
speak for the silence between the stars.

3.

I apologize for my dialogues with the light.
I apologize for the voices in the red hibiscus.
I apologize for the small details still
discernible in the sparse grass of the yard.
I apologize for the birds that would not nest
in the absent dark of the tree,
for the long evenings, and the square
of sun on the bark of the tree, and the promise
that prevented the last hours.
I apologize for the leaves moving
like carbon copies of leaves across your face.

CARP

∾

Just as you walk out of the Japanese garden
you find two huge stones—one standing,
the other lying down like a tired man—with some
vaguely aesthetic purpose in mind.
You think: They are probably pondering their next
move, how they will reposition themselves.
If you stand behind them you can see the Los
Angeles skyline rising as if for the first time,
as if it didn't exist from any other angle.
You have just chosen between a woman
and a future that is sometimes as uncertain
as the purpose of these stones. You have decided
how you will make your next move. You
have seen the sun falling through the rising
skyline. An image of the woman you will leave
begins to swim inside you like wrong blood,
like your own blood suddenly turned to water.
You can't quite say it, can you? No. Not even
to yourself. She was, after all, your only
way of measuring the world. Now the world
is a thing without proportions. Even dusk becomes
a difficult task—how to look at it, what
to expect, what to make of the light between
two buildings, the soft light on these
stones which have yet to make their moves.
You have stared into the heart of the light
from the safety of your dark glasses.
But the world, you have thought all along.
The world. And you wonder how you could have
decided what to take with you for the rest
of your life, what to leave behind. To steer
a life in a single walk from the street
to the bottom of the garden where bamboo

clusters at the source of the stream.
You looked into the clear water. The carp
were serene and fragile. She would have never
noticed, you thought. She would have said:
Fish. I hate fish. And you would have taken
her hand, tried to explain the importance
of color as camouflage—how certain insects
could be waiting there, on the leaves; how they
may have become her idea of leaves. You
thought of this, of how she would have turned
the color of water or falling sun. You thought
of the carp—how they die because the world
has become too large for them, how the world
grows a little smaller each time one
of them dies and rises and turns to water.

COLE PORTER

~∞~

Tell them something you can live with.

The world is a hyperbole of grief.

Say *Grief* and give them magic.
Your sleight of hand
is all they need to understand that magic
is its own hyperbole,
that the world they've been banking on
is going out of business—*Sale
of the Century* across each window,
the mannequins half stripped, the windows
half empty. You at the door, handing
out coupons for anything. You

at the door, talking the language
of the restless. Because it sounds good.
Or because there's always a market
for love in an age of discontent.

Let them bank on that.

Rob them clean. Sell them back
their own dreams and live on the profit.
Say *Bargain.* Say *Your money
or your heart.*

ALTRUISM

꘎

I'd give you my seat, but I'm sitting here.
—CHICO TO GROUCHO MARX, IN *A NIGHT AT THE OPERA*

Everything we know about death
is not enough to kill us. It's the last good season
of tourism and exile and I have a window seat
on the bus to the hotel. Beside me
is a man who refuses medical assistance,
claiming his god will intercede. They can't tell us
apart. That in itself is a considerable
blow to the gut of the revolution.
When they searched our bags, they missed
the huge shell I found half-buried in the sand.
At the hotel, I show it to the guard who
counts his paces on the other
side of the barbed wire. He's dying
without medical or divine intercession.
He mentions a wife, a daughter,
a garden with alternating rows
of lettuce and seashells. If the authorities
try to confiscate my shell, he suggests
that I tell them I'm dying.
Or dead, if I can get away with it. He points
to the bus parked outside, the dying man
waving from his window seat.
The guard says that if I bring the shell
to my ear, I can hear myself leaving again.

VALERIE MARTÍNEZ

NIGHT OF FATHERS

‿❦‿

I have come at the wish of my heart
from the pool of Double Fire. . . .
Give to me my mouth [that] I may speak
with it. May I follow my heart at its
season of fire and night.
— FROM *THE EGYPTIAN BOOK OF THE DEAD*

Like a dragged gem, floating,
   the tethers holding me
over the fields of ill, farewell.
   Toward the region beyond, gone

out of my body. No more heart,
   no thighs to shiver,
recesses of hurt. To the sun
   moving through corn and wheat.
The table with water and cakes.
   The elaborate feast we imagine

And the limbs coming back, there,
   like the wished, small animals
come home. And the forms sorrow takes:
   winds, rains, the bursts
of nature. Reclaiming:

   the red pump, all artery, chamber,
the palms and wrists indented
   with the shapes of new things.
The inner thighs so sweet,
   their little white marks.

And the forms the memory takes—
   dreams of iron weight, doves

flying in the belly, wings furious.
　　Waters, waters, pools
at the horizon of eyes.

And the mouth given, flying back
　　to the face, the last,
the dangerous, for see how it wants,
　　how remembers. Curved bow
holds the shapes of sufferings,
　　those fathers. And the lover's
weakness, places. Then, plummeting

　　back to the lived. Mouth
now emptied of lies must take us back
　　to the old dwelling places:
the hurt, earth, hurt beautiful.

THE HUMAN UNIVERSE

∾∾

What is broken   opened
   like the sun
   on the sugar cane
like a wave of heat
over grass huts and children
   with wire cars
   sticks and old tires
is the heart
Opened

to everything
   made of heat   regret
   delight   passion
the agony of someone's luck
   and some terror

I saw this
It was the story of a man
   who cheated
   then raged upon his wife
the kindness of women
who nursed her health
   It took place
   in a village
the size of most people's houses
a microcosm
   from there to here
   endless

I am learning
   about the shattering
   the constant unfolding

of this essence within us
I had to learn it
    in the summer
    below the equator
understand it has occurred
forever as I remember

You have broken something
in me
    the village of my heart
    disintegrates in the heat
and Father
with his tentative hands
    comes running

    What is eternal
    what is ever
blooming in the sun
of the human universe

    rage and tenderness
    rage and tenderness.

TESORO

~o~

for Timothy Trujillo, 1951–91

Just a few years ago, when everything was permanent.
Or on the edge of. Or, yes, perhaps over the edge,
or falling away from . . .

Was like the façades of the Sagrada Familia with their
delicate foliage, swans, turtles bearing the weight of.
Everything alive and carved out of stone.

It was my treasure, this permanence, the architecture
of living. Everything stone-true and buttressed:
arc and arc and arc of an ancient city.

Can you guess what will come next? Can you?
Touching you like the sheerest handkerchief of silk?
When the beloveds fell from the sky and disappeared?
From stone to diaphanous silk. On the wind. Sudden.

It was a mistake, amiss. It was perception
of what is light as what is heavy, and permanent.
Sometimes, one's hand can pass through stone,
and it is not a dream.

One got sick, and another, another.
Someone I loved, who loved me, disappeared.

Two, or is it three, who died. This
is honest enough, enough to say bluntly.
This is for Tim.

In "The Visitation" it is beautiful:
the handmaid's arms are barely covered,
delicate skin beneath transparent silk.

CHILDREN OF THE DISAPPEARED

꘎

(Argentina)

The curved pelvic bone dug up,
showing childbirth before death.
The bullet hole near the top of the skull.

The boy misbehaves, arrives home
covered with petals and mud.
Unearthed from the neighbor's flower bed.
He gets the back of the hand several times.
She tells him he's a brat.
She tells him he's a burden
she can't bear. Later,
she throws her delicate hairbrush
through a window of the house.
Her husband goes for her neck,
for her hands. She calls him a murderer
who shot the child's mother.
She can't tolerate the boy,
won't tolerate what isn't really hers
any longer. Better to be barren.

The boy's room is like a womb
with too many windows. Half-awake,
he lies on the good cheek remembering
the garden. Hears *mother . . . longer.*
Sees white worms, petals in a pile of earth.
He is looking for treasures:
flint, animal bones, obsidian, iron.
A door slams. Someone—Mother?—
is shouting somewhere.
He dreams the front door opening,

the porch superimposed on the flower bed,
spilling out. A woman he doesn't know
at the door, hand to mouth, calling
. . . *home now,*
come now,
find your way home.

ABSENCE, LUMINESCENT

~o~

1.

Arch inverted: white peony
and stamens, yellow. Center
of the body. Imagines.
Who is absent.

Fingers in my mouth—memory.
Dragonfly so blue in the head.
Orange, as fire, in the body.

Wings, transparence. Disappearing arms.

The space where he was. Aureole.
The space he is, she was.
And the opposite.

Defines the dragon who flies.
Iridescent where it was, is.
Echo of hued wings.

2.

Heat at the center. Heat where
she was. Lack of passion where
the torso

won't go. No path through
what is occupied. Space.

3.

Falls in a delicate arch, sees
own soul. Cadaver as shrine,
concavity.
So white. Says white flesh
and no spirit.

And touching the dead.
And touching what is not.

4.

In our calculations: the fact
of matter at lack of matter.
The invisible, collapsed star.
If you must, a "black hole."
Thus the message of blackness
clearly signaling the coordinates
of nothingness.

5.

Remembers the pilgrimage
to the illumined wall.
And Christ's face was said to appear.

God's face. Who sees it?
Child trying, trying.

Says to the child
(and it's the juncture):
go toward faith, go through absence,
way to belief.

6.

(Not believing. Not seeing and
not believing. All the chants
to atmosphere, blanks.)

7.

Implodes, and all the way to nothing.
To illumine, first, then fades to black.
Hole where light was.
Absent star, perforation in there.

And memory of light, halo on.
Angels who walk among. Seeming
darkness around the head.

Falling languid. Lover not there.

"My sweet: the miles, the night."

"Darling my fingernails bear their half-
moons half-gone how long . . ."

"The house, really my love, the rooms.
They're emptied, haunted."

"Ghost of you come here body."

And I can see her, worshipper,
with a blue robe biting her nails—
thinks it's true, true,
someone witnessed the miracles—
someone saw it all.

And the mouths, reeling the bass in.
Hook out the parabola of mouth air.
Violence of fish body in the air.
Absence of water, presence of . . .

Open my mouth—his fingers going in.
The gills going open open nothing nothing.

Dragonfly so blue in the head.
On red wings, disappeared.

Sing sing going going.

12.

Of all the tendernesses at the end
there was the constant ritual the washing
the turning of the body so cleansed
by a lover's hands until the struggle
for breath the gasp and the body
getting less warm the ceremony and like
the Egyptians all the preparation
then the emerging presence the advent
of absence the adornments, artifacts
in the tombs where the lungs tighten
in our awe it's all there but spirit
said *goodbye are you gone it's difficult*
to tell you must be.

13.

Theoretically, everything must be seen
as negative space. And then the task
of mistrust, tackled head on.
There are limits to the five mortal
senses. No limits beyond.

They said.

14.

Reunified through occupied
space. Hands at my lips.

Explosion of black in the opened
mouth. Five fingers toward

the perforation, through dark
hair. Toward the void, toward
the presence in there.

THE NEW WORLD

You are the kind of beauty
which delivers me up
to some midnight vision of water—
dark, enigmatic, moving with figures
so exotic they must be ancient animals.
Somehow it happens that the new world
emerges out of restlessness,
the sleepless turning of colors
in darkness. This is about love
and not insomnia, about belonging
and not the blackmares of evening.
The animals are gentle, like sweet mothers,
bold as fiesty amazons, and there I am
looking like a pharaoh's queen,
abstract and beautiful.
I couldn't tell whether I was asleep
or waking, but this came
after a memory of you
slicing open a wild cucumber
to reveal the cool, orange pulp.
It was southern Africa, hot.
Your hair was cut too short,
like a boy's, and it was illegal
to play with nature by cutting.
But I wanted to see, wanted
even more than the white rhinos
and newborn ostriches,
the young elephants up close.
It was blooming from the vine
like a drop of green water.
And nothing stopped you
from granting my wish,

nothing, nothing.
It was how much you wanted,
for my desire,
how many images you've cut
open, O Love, for me.

THE RELIQUARIES

Seaside, and the fragment of one running—
calves, ribs, gray eyes into water.
There he goes. Waves. Then buoying up
as into sky. And the seagulls fly,
seeing it as relief, a story. Once

they were there, two on a white blanket.
The circumference of a shadow. Sunlight
around that shadow. The relation of two:
bathers, robed figures, configured as one.
As if she touches him—tender—and it is done.

(I've gone back to it. I've, I've—
it's not where I am. I give it away again.)
You're there. It's still in the sand.
It's trying to chisel it down.

How it comes forth: story.
Wanting it, carving it down to a vision.
Architecture, a coliseum of bent light,
the beautiful scatter of broken stones.
(I can turn it into stones.)
Love, love: a portico, a labyrinth.

And his simple aquatics, legs and arms
in the brackish, littered with white fish.
The song, under there, of how he leaves
and naturally, like all the living things:
animals, summer, daylight for the eves.

And the buildings, all shadows and beings:
block, angels, curve. With the love,

memory of all loves. The pediments,
our reliquaries.

It's our landscape, artifact—it might hurt.
(Run to, run away from it.)

TRAVELER

∽

Everything she wants she sees
in the coin of this dark child's eye.

Desire lives in her like the secret
of the statue-goddess,
when man mistakes her for a fetish.

It isn't that she's felt nothing
in those hollows: heart & pelvis.

Just that the orphan is asking her
with a look of wishes & desire,
a look crying mother-savior.

It could occur anywhere
but does so finally here

in the sugar fields, among the stalks
where she finds him
sucking cane in the harvest season.

And everything, all of life itself
is gathered here for one second, endless.

He calls to her, his eyes go blind
in the sun and every absent meal,
vicious cane snake, wish for beauty,

wish for beauty's reprieve,
enters her like sweetness
and riches and thunder.

Big Bend, Swaziland

IT IS NOT

⋙

We have the body of a woman, an arch over the ground,
but there is no danger. Her hair falls, spine bowed,
but no one is with her. The desert, yes, with its
cacti, bursage, sidewinders. She is not in danger.
If we notice, there are the tracks of animals
moving east, toward the sunrise, and the light
is about to touch a woman's body without possession.
Here, there are no girls' bones in the earth, marked
with violence. A cholla blooms, just two feet away.
It blooms.

There is a man, like her father, who wakes to a note
saying *I have gone for a day, to the desert.* Now,
he believes she is in danger. He will try to anticipate
what happens to a young woman, how it will happen, how
he will deal with the terrible. In him, he feels
he knows this, somehow, he knows because there are men
he knows who are capable. This place she has gone, where?
But it doesn't matter. There is, first of all, the heat
which scorches, snakes with their coils and open mouths,
men who go there with the very thing in mind. The very
thing.

It is the desert on its own. Miles. Beyond what anyone
can see. Not peaceful nor vengeful. It does not bow down.
It is not danger. I cannot speak of it without easing
or troubling myself. It is not panorama nor theater.
I do not know. It is only conception: then fruits
like gifts or burdens I bear. Whether arch, a prayer,
or danger. They can happen, yes, we conceive them.
This very woman I know, the man does sit tortured.
The desert, created, embodies its place, and watch us
lay our visions, o God, upon it.

NOCTURNE

To the interior, limbs folded,
happens inside, the ankle bent like weep.
It's the body, attitude of darkness,
eyes on the sorry, sorry. Awake,
so far away. Like a ghost.
And the song in the street, distant
trill, aria. Some enormous pomp.
While the ravens shine on, and all
the streetlights. While the scorpion
holds its anger, ready ready.

In the eyes, once, the neck.
Swathed green, turquoise, aquamarine,
black. Like the six scarves at the window.
The prism of scarves. The mouth
resting in the valley of nerves.
How it turns: the teeth just there,
the windows with their screens and bellows.
The word on the sharpest edge,
undoes, leaves.

And how the hands go hold up,
filter the yellow autumn night.
Find the sweet notes—sing
gone, gone, it's how, it's home.

GLORIA VANDO

IN THE DARK BACKWARD

for Nina

How is it I was not raised
on the riverfront block
with the tall trees and a tall woman
calling my name, the sweetness
of warm peaches on her breath,
her arms like soft vowels
cushioning me from death? Why
is it I was confined to night,
forced to travel the shaft tunnel
below Manhattan before alighting
blonde and blue-eyed in Washington
Heights, where your mother
would add another plate for supper
and, long after the sun
had painted the Palisades across
the Hudson a deep bronze, wonder
aloud if I would be going soon?
I would pretend I had not heard
so I could stay until the moon
rose over the cliffs, when we'd
slip out and walk across
the bridge (only one level then)
to the Jersey side where we'd sit
on the rocks to talk and watch
the early morning light patch up
the city's wounds. Was it Godly spite
that bore me to the wrong block
far from your haven on Haven Avenue—
or was it luck that locked

me in that dry-dock, where nothing but
my mind could billow in the breeze,
and only the cries of lonelier
children, like windswept echoes from
a ghost ship, could free my grief.

MY MOTHER CUNNING, YET INNOCENT

My mother cunning, yet innocent
Grabbing the new moon by its promise
And whistling through the suave sky
For an easy escape to where stardom
Should have been but seldom was.

My mother split like a seasoned log
Ready for burning, yet whole and immutable
As bronze, her slender arms unbendable,
Her teeth clenched behind
An ardent Rita Hayworth smile.

Still ill-defined, she slips away,
Gathering herself up into the thinnest
Sliver of equivocation, falling
Between folds of supple logic until
She's almost out of earshot.
But I'm obsessed with the mystery,
Shout after her *Wait! Wait!*

The air is heavy with gardenia and sweet
Tobacco. Smoke rings from her lips
Drift out of sight like elliptic vows
While I strain to capture them
On my tiny wrists and fingers
Not knowing then, no, not yet knowing—
trusting her to be mine forever.

FATHER'S DAY

～◦～

This time his father takes him
to the Liberty Memorial,
a World War I monument
overlooking the city. In single
file they climb the spiral
staircase, the boy's legs
straining to reach the last step.
Swell way to spend a Sunday,
his father had said, and
the boy feels proud to be
on top of the world with his dad.
The man leans over as if to kiss
him, the boy lifts his face
expectantly—suddenly he's upside
down and before he can resist
his father's fists around
his ankles he's dangling over
the side of the tower, dangling
like a tangled marionette above
the coaxing ground, his red
jacket, like a spurt of blood,
coating his head and arms
as they bang against the granite.
Coins from his pockets sprinkle
the earth with tiny setting suns.
You can always trust me, son—
his father's words bruise the air—
always, you hear? He feels
his heart pummeling his eyes
and ears, warm urine caressing
his chest. *Yes, Daddy, yes*—
he cries back, his voice

threadbare over the shivering
treetops—*yes, yes*—trying
to penetrate his father's glazed
senses—*yes, yes*—hoping
to reassure him once and for all
so he will stop having to prove
his love.

IN THE CREVICES OF NIGHT

There's a man in my dream
a man with a hatchet
ransacking my bureau
hacking at the doll asleep
in the bottom drawer.

A bloodless ritual.

He calls himself a surgeon, says
he's up on the latest laser beam
techniques. I know better.
I know the jig's up.
Youth is waning and the end
is closing in on the beginning—
a telescopic fantasy focused
on dismembered limbs, a glass eye
rolling across the parquet floor,
tiny fingernails scattered
in my underwear scratching
at the obscenity of early death.
But not a drop of blood. Not a cry.

I turn from the dream
and pressing my body to yours
reach for you
across the thin ice of night.

COMMONWEALTH, COMMON POVERTY

∞

for Zoltan Sumonyi

A visitor comes from Hungary as from outer space,
Dropping into my Midwestern world with poems
About himself and that bracketed place he hails from.
And though the gift he brings is veiled, submerged
In allegory and myth, I recognize myself. Say
To him: this poem you read is about me. He smirks.

He has read his poems before and not been heard.
He is weary, somewhat cavalier. His body is taut like
A gymnast's. His eyes form flat, black mirrors of distrust.
Adjusting to what he perceives as enemy turf. It's August.
He sheds his jacket, rolls his sleeves above his biceps.
A pulse in his temple keeps rhythm with his words.

He tries again, leads me as he reads. I see us both,
Two generations earlier—perhaps three—running down once
Familiar streets with new strange names and I am plagued
By what I might have been had nothing changed,
Had Teddy's boys not made it to the top of San Juan
Hill. Like him I, too, yearn for connections

Between my parents' world and this one, long for
A tie cut short by strangers—does it matter
That his were Russian, mine American, or that
His lines allude to Greeks and gifts of death, while
Mine—because our history is yet to be revamped—
Still lament the Massacre of Ponce? Here we sit

In a Kansas City motel, hearing what we say
Translated by a man we have to trust—could be

A friend, could be a secret agent—a clean-cut man
In a banker's suit who keeps his jacket on,
Claims he walked from Budapest to freedom, and
Converts our pain into passionless sounds. Yes,

Here we sit, feeling as our ancestors surely felt
The day their world shifted in its global socket
And everything they cherished perished in the quake,
Leaving them disfranchised, disconnected from
Their past, from each other, from themselves. How
They must have searched then for a look, a gesture,

A familiar world to ease their terror, the arch of a brow,
A jawline—*something* to bind them to their captors,
Something so slight it might have gone unnoticed
Had all remained whole. And we, their progeny, now
Sit here immersed in Russian and American symbols:
We, their future, have become what they most feared.

SWALLOWS OF SALANGAN

❧

Morton Feldman Dies at 61;
An Experimental Composer
— THE NEW YORK TIMES

Sixty-one? I thought you were that back
then when you first lumbered into our
lives "like a bear," my daughter said,
clutching hers and giving up her bed
without an argument. An owl, I thought,
observing two tufts of slick, brown hair
hanging free like weary horns; eyes intense,
intimidating, behind the thickest lenses
I had ever seen, then suddenly small,
glasses raised, scanning the inch-close
page with laser speed. It was summer
that March in Corpus Christi. A scent
of jasmine and moist tweed slipped past
you into the kitchen mingling at random
with the bacon and the coffee. Crumbs
from your lips added an aleatory voice
to the graph paper score you hummed:
you were making history at my breakfast
table and I, Clio, was feeding you honey.
Only your music was minimal. I was

impressed. Not only by your presence
but what you left with me, what stayed,
permeating the bones of memory until today
when I play your records at the library,
huge headphones holding pieces of the past
together in a vise of sound—sound, Morty,
your sound—disquieting, "getting

under the seat" as you had warned, yet
reverential, hushed, as if in mourning
for itself. Once, in Houston—remember?—
washes of that sound, a voix céleste
like a swell of keening swallows filled
the Rothko Chapel you honored, hallowing
the art, the chapel and all therein. Now
a scant two decades later, you are dead

and much is made of disillusion. But
it wasn't you or your music or the media
hype—perhaps the hype—that led
to disillusion, what my father maintained
is the worst thing that could happen.
Something sinister shortened America's
attention span to 30 screaming minutes,
the reading line to 19 picas, hemlines
to the crotch. This is a time of expedience,
of shrink-wrapped identical portions. No
foreplay. No afterthought. Get on with it.
And you, freed from "the intrinsic morality
of the medium," creating your own morality
with a four-and-one-half-hour string quartet
that ended to an almost empty hall—Ah,

where to preserve your innocence, Morty,
in a cage, under glass, the wolf at the door?
Had you forgotten that 4′ 33″ of silence
was more than our culture could endure?
Even then, back then, my friend, when
you were Schubert to a flower generation.

KNIFE

∾∘∾

She was old. She lived alone in a small house
two blocks away. When they found her, days after,
she had been stabbed seventeen times—as if
a host of assassins had struck an empress down.
She might have even looked up briefly
before the final cut, spurting blood and
an imperious last line or two. Perhaps not.
Perhaps the first wound had done the trick—
the rest sport for the mad or wicked. A handyman
lived nearby. He worked odd jobs while leading
a secret life with his neighbor's Anglo wife,
who would sneak him in when her husband
and her son were out. No one questioned
Sánchez about the old lady. He traveled alone.
This was a gang job. One day while walking past
a vacant lot close by the boy spots a shiny
object winking at him through layers of rust
like a cheap sequin—summoning him to stoop
down, swoop it up, later to brandish it
with pride before his mother's sucked
astonishment. Give it here, she says.
The name on the crudely carved handle is clear,
letters printed in black Magic Marker—but
are they clearly the handyman's? Sánchez
is a common name. She knows he doesn't stand
a chance if he stands trial. Knows they'll find
guilt hidden like stacks of money unexplained
beneath the floorboards of his mind. She knows
Texas. Knows how stuff gets planted when you're
a Mexican without an alibi and they need
a solution. And most of all she knows, knows
as she digs the tiny grave for the homemade knife,

knows as she pats the soil over it and sows
the seeds of justice, knows as she pours
a 50-50 mixture of water and fish emulsion
over it to make the seeds grow, knows, damn it,
she just knows that he is guilty as hell.

LYDIA'S PHANTASMAGORIA

And tonight's headline news:
All of Puerto Rico watches as TV's Queen of Soaps
is condemned to life imprisonment. Stay tuned.

High,
like when you're in a glass elevator going up
and you feel stationary
and everything around you seems to be going down,
dropping,
slipping slowly away:
the light switch slinking down the wall, the vase
full of flowers sinking beneath the painting
over the mantel, the Ralph Goings painting of a woman—
could be any woman, though he calls her Shanna,
sitting at a Kentucky Fried Chicken window booth—
a woman left suddenly, left alone,
left incomplete as though half of her had fallen
away, disappeared out of sight,
the two cups of coffee on the table unsipped, growing
clotted and cool like the relationship,
the cigarette between her fingers
no longer sparkling, but smouldering imperceptibly
like the one who left, is left, and
the cross-legged woman left behind reworks,
rephrases the parting words,
restructures, relives the final scene,
repossesses what may or may not have been said (she
can't remember), so that it hurts less,
maybe even comes out right
with a musical comedy ending of forever
and ever amen and all that crap and caramba.
But it's not that way—not that time,

not this time, not then, not now, not ever, and
the word that can heal gets mislaid, misfired,
feelings misstated, misconstrued,
justice miscarried, sometimes all the way to the chair,
and not the one looking out from
Colonel Sanders' place—that's art, that's fiction,
this is life, death. This is murder.

In the beginning . . . hell, there is no beginning,
only a question and answer period to start
and the questions are loaded and the answers are invariably wrong
and these two, like the couple in the Goings painting,
they tried—we *all* try.
The story goes (and I have no reason to doubt it)
that Lydia did him in—
that one night while making love—a long time coming round,
too long—Luis made the fatal slip, calling her
by the other one's name.
Had she still been in the throes of ecstasy
his *Nydia* might have sneaked by undetected,
but as patience would have it, she heard,
stiffened beneath him,
her body hard and flat and dry;
his, finally spent, sprawling like a lead sheet
across the glass bones of her rage. In that moment
she knew he had deceived her
and knowing,
waited,
waited until the time was right,
playing at the game of love while playing for time,
not yet knowing what to do
but knowing something had to be done, someone
done in.
She plotted in the only way she knew—Dantesquely
fitting the punishment to the crime.
She hired three (already a mistake, a stupid mistake,
$3 \times 2 = 6$ too many

involved, too many palms to grease,
bucks to pass) thugs, hired three thugs to kill him.
But first the slow revenge—intense,
steady—because death after all is liberation,
slow revenge is pain: an imprisonment of self
within self, a double jeopardy of torture.
Satisfied, she rubbed her hands with wicked glee
and laughed *¡Ja! ¡Ja!* adding
the Spanish equivalent of "you bastard, you'll moan
and groan for *me* before I'm through!" *(Hijo de la gran . . . et
cetera.)*

On January 6th the three thugs—kings for a day—
kidnap him and deliver him blindfolded
to a nondescript, out-of-the-way room
in a bourgeois suburb of San Juan
that smells of *chorizos* and *habichuelas.*
Miramar without a view—no ocean, no sky, no moon, no place
for the reigning stars of Puerto Rican soaps to be caught dead in.
And, waiting for him, his patient wife—
legs crossed, cigarette smouldering like the one
in the painting—eye ready behind
an instantaneously gratifying
Kodakcolorpolaroid,
its protruding flashbulb palpitating
like a stud in heat—ready to document the brilliant defeat
of Luis in particular, man in general, ready to
show him falling from dignity,
from hope, from grace,
from the top of the popularity polls *(click!)*
falling *(click!)* to ignominy and low, low ratings.
And she ascending on that elevator
getting high, higher,
snapping and flashing
picture *(click!)* after picture
of his long, slow descent.
He might have stepped backwards out of an open window

on the 31st floor of the CBS building
and fallen to his death in 5 and 9/10 of a second,
but instead he is snapped up,
snapped over and over again, his wounds hissing
in vivid color,
his tiny parts removed one by one—
a nail *(click!)*, an earlobe *(click!)*,
a testicle *(click! click! click! click! click!)*—
missing except in the snapshots strewn face up
across the bloodsoaked bittersweet shag carpet.
And Luis missing the good lines,
missing the applause—
Oh baby missing you-oo-oo-oo, oh baby missing you-hooo-oo—
missing all but the last laugh—
between *socorros* (Pietà never had it so good)
he damns her and curses her and spites her
with cries for Nydia! Nydia! Nydia!
which sound to her like the *nya-nya-nyaaaah*
of vengeful siblings,
and suddenly Lydia feels his anguish, his anger.
Sees his hatred.
And to shut out a reflection of her own loathsomeness,
she orders the three assassins
to pluck out his eyes *(click! click!)*.
Nearly out of film she has them stuff his body
into his car, douse it with gasoline,
set it on fire. Strains of *aguinaldos* drift in
through the open window—*abrir la puerta al niño
que está pidiendo amparo* . . . et cetera.

Steadying the camera on the second-story window ledge,
the craggy bricks carving deep ridges into her elbows,
she snaps the final spectacle from above.
And Lydia becomes the flames—
teasing, playful, at first—her fingers
combing the fringes of the orange floral bedspread,
pulling off each petal—

he loves me, he loves me not—
unfolding each leaf, each bud, her tongue
reading his skin like Braille—every pore,
every mole, every tangled curl telling a different story,
spelling a new name—
he loves her, he loves me not.
As the flames rise
higher and higher past her window
she tilts the camera up toward the soiled sky,
and all at once feels herself
sinking irreversibly
as though she were on an elevator
plummeting
through the earth's mantle,
deep, deep into the magma of memory,
beyond hope, beyond redemption,
beyond *revision*, watching everything,
everything she had ever wanted,
everything she had ever loved, evanesce—
watching her whole life
go up in smoke.

TRAILER: *Tune in next week to the first episode*
of Love and Murder: On Screen and Off, *featuring*
that hot new sensation Nydia Estrella,
in the title role of Lydia (click! click! click!).

Habichuelas: beans.
Aguinaldos: Christmas carols.
Abrir la puerta al niño que está pidiendo amparo: open the door to the
(Christ) child who's asking for help.

BLANCA'S RED LIPS

ᙎᙙ

This wedding in Lawrence,
is like most others except when it's over
the bride and groom get a standing
ovation, as if they were the ingenues
in a hit play with a happy ending.
An earlier wedding intrudes and I see
my friend Blanca jumping up and down
like a small child chanting *Yes! Yes!*
the groom's cheeks puffed with laughter,
the priest asking the congregation
to join him in a round of applause for
this special couple who, after ten years
of equivocating and playing the field,
chose to play it safe and get saved, *saved*—
and Blanca, her mouth a perfect oval of joy.
Then my sister's shower a year later,
the male stripper gyrating hips against air,
women snapping telephotos for a closer
look in the privacy of their own lens,
and Blanca, that same glaring smile,
ululating at his hard, false promise—
already knowing, even then knowing—
and we too busy asking tired questions
about babies and when, as though
we had a right to know, and just weeks
later my daughter's voice on the machine,
    sobbing, sobbing,
Blanca's red lips seared into my memory.

for Blanca, who died of AIDS

ODE TO YOUR BACK

The days wrap themselves around me
like worn shawls.
I am cold, always
on the point of shivering.

Nights come stunted and maimed,
undernourished children
with no place to go.

This night I dream of happy
endings: the hero, turbaned, rouged,
made up with heart-shaped lips, penciled
brows, married to the ingenue
to keep her safe because he loves
is not in love with her and

wake to find us, you and me
and the war-orphaned babies in London
who died from lack of touch
and my own chilled body moving
moving in close to the heat

of your back. Your back.

CONTRIBUTORS

SANDRA M. CASTILLO's poems have appeared in numerous journals and anthologies, including *Paper Dance: 52 Latino Poets* (Persea Books) and *A Century of Cuban Writers in Florida* (Pineapple Press). She teaches at Dade Community College in Florida.

LORNA DEE CERVANTES is the author of two books of poetry, *Emplumada* (University of Pittsburgh Press) and *From the Cables of Genocide: Poems on Love and Hunger* (Arte Publico Press). She has received numerous awards, including a grant from the National Endowment for the Arts, the Paterson Poetry Prize, and a Lila Wallace Reader's Digest Fund major fellowship. Her work has appeared in many journals and anthologies, including *The Norton Anthology of Poetry*, *After Aztlán: Latino Poets in the Nineties* (David R. Godine) and *In Other Words: Literature by Latinas of the United States* (Arte Publico Press). She has been a visiting scholar at the University of Houston and currently teaches creative writing at the University of Colorado in Boulder.

JUDITH ORTIZ COFER is the author of a novel, *The Line of the Sun* (University of Georgia Press); a memoir, *Silent Dancing* (Arte Publico Press); and three poetry collections, *Terms of Survival, Reaching for the Mainland* (both Bilingual Press) and *The Latin Deli* (University of Georgia Press). She has received several writing fellowships, including ones from the National Endowment for the Arts and the Winner Bynner Foundation for Poetry. She is a professor of English and creative writing at the University of Georgia in Athens.

VICTOR HERNÁNDEZ CRUZ is the author of several collections of poetry, including *Snaps* (Random House), *By Lingual Wholes* (Momos Press), *Selected Poems* (Arte Publico Press), and two volumes from Coffee House Press, *Red Beans* and *Panoramas*. *Red Beans* received a Publishers Weekly Ten Best Books of the Year Award. Cruz was a featured poet on Bill Moyers's *Language of Life* series, and has been a two-time champion in the Taos Heavyweight Poetry Bout. His numerous awards include fellowships from the National Endowment for the Arts and the Guggenheim Foundation. He has been a visiting professor at the University of California at Berkeley and at San Diego, the

University of Michigan, and the University of Colorado in Boulder. He lives in Aguas Buenas, a town on his native island of Puerto Rico.

SILVIA CURBELO was born in Matanzas, Cuba, in 1955 and emigrated to the United States in 1967. She is the author of a chapbook of poems, *The Geography of Leaving* (Silverfish Review Press), and a full-length collection, *The Secret History of Water* (Anhinga Press). Her work has appeared in numerous journals, including *The Kenyon Review, Prairie Schooner, The Bloomsbury Review,* and *Caliban.* She is the recipient of poetry fellowships from the National Endowment for the Arts, the Cintas Foundation, the Florida Arts Council, and an Atlantic Center for the Arts Cultural Exchange Fellowship to La Napoule Arts Foundation in France. She lives in Tampa, Florida.

JUAN DELGADO is the author of a chapbook of poems, *Working On It* (Chicano Chapbook Series, Berkeley), and a full-length collection, *Green Web* (University of Georgia Press). His poems have appeared in several journals, including *The Missouri Review, The Connecticut Poetry Review,* and *Alchemy.* His awards include the Chicano Literary Prize at the University of California at Irvine and the University Educator of the Year Award from the Association of Mexican American Educators. He teaches at California State University in San Bernardino.

MARTÍN ESPADA is the author of five poetry collections, most recently *Imagine the Angels of Bread* (W. W. Norton), nominated for the National Book Critics Circle Award. A previous book, *Rebellion Is the Circle of a Lover's Hands* (Curbstone Press), was awarded both the Paterson Poetry Prize and the PEN/Revson Fellowship. His poems have appeared in *Harper's, The Nation, The New York Times Book Review,* and *The Best American Poetry,* among other journals. He is the editor of *Poetry Like Bread: Poets of the Political Imagination* (Curbstone Press) and *El Coro: A Chorus of Latino and Latina Poets* (University of Massachusetts Press). A former tenant lawyer, he teaches literature at the University of Massachusetts in Amherst.

DIANA GARCÍA's poetry has appeared in several journals, including *The Kenyon Review, Ploughshares, 13th Moon,* and *The Mid-American Review.* A native of California's San Joaquin Valley, she divides her time between her home in San Diego, California, and New Britain, Connecticut. She teaches literature at Central Connecticut State University.

RICHARD GARCÍA is the author of *The Flying Garcia* (University of Pittsburgh Press) and a bilingual children's book, *My Aunt Otila's Spirits* (Children's Book Press). He has received fellowships from the National Endowment for the Arts and the California Arts Council. His journal awards include the Cohen Award from *Ploughshares* magazine and the Greensboro Award from *The Greensboro Review*. His work has appeared in *The Kenyon Review, The Colorado Review, The Gettysburg Review,* and other journals. He is poet-in-residence at Children's Hospital in Los Angeles, California.

RAY GONZÁLEZ is the author of *Memory Fever: A Journey beyond El Paso del Norte* (Broken Moon Press), a memoir about growing up in the Southwest. He is the author of five books of poetry, including *Twilights and Chants* (James Andrews and Company), *The Heat of Arrivals* (BOA Editions), and *Cabato Sentora* (BOA Editions). He is the editor of twelve anthologies, including *Muy Macho: Latino Men Confront Their Manhood* (Anchor/Doubleday) and *Currents from the Dancing River: Contemporary Latino Poetry, Fiction, and Essays* (Harcourt, Brace). I Ie received a 1988 Colorado Governor's Award for Excellence in the Arts and a 1993 Before Columbus Foundation American Book Award for Excellence in Editing. He is assistant professor of English and Latin American Studies at the University of Illinois in Chicago.

MAURICE KILWEIN GUEVARA is the author of two books of poetry, *Postmortem* (University of Georgia Press) and *Poems of the River Spirit* (University of Pittsburgh Press). His work has appeared in *Poetry, The Kenyon Review, Exquisite Corpse, Parnassus,* and other journals. He has received awards from the Bread Loaf Writers' Conference, the J. William Fulbright Commission, the Pennsylvania Council on the Arts, and the Pennsylvania Humanities Council. He teaches creative writing and performance art at Indiana University of Pennsylvania.

JUAN FELIPE HERRERA is the author of a memoir, *Mayan Drifter: Chicano Poet of the Lowlands of America* (Temple University Press), and eight books of poetry. They include *Facegames* (As Is, So & So Press), winner of a Before Columbus American Book Award, *Akrilica* (Alcatraz Editions), *Night Train to Tuxtla* (University of Arizona Press), and *Love among the Riots* (Curbstone Press). His essays and stories are included in the anthologies *Muy Macho: Latino Men Confront Their Manhood* (Anchor/Doubleday) and *Mirrors Beneath the Earth: Chicano Short Fiction* (Curbstone Press). He has been the recipient of fellowships from the National Endowment for the Arts and the California Arts Council. His best-selling children's book *Calling the Doves* (Children's Press) has received numerous awards. He is associate professor of Chicano and Latin American Studies at California State University in Fresno.

DIONISIO D. MARTÍNEZ was born in Cuba in 1956. He is the author of three collections of poetry—*Bad Alchemy* (W. W. Norton), *History as a Second Language* (Ohio State University Press), and the chapbook *Dancing at the Chelsea* (State Street Press). He is the recipient of a National Endowment for the Arts fellowship and a Whiting Writer's Award. His work has been widely published in journals and anthologies, including *The Norton Anthology of Poetry* and *The Best American Poetry 1992* and *1994* (Scribner). He lives in Tampa, Florida, where he is an affiliate writer of the Writer's Voice of the YMCA.

VALERIE MARTÍNEZ lived in Swaziland, Africa, from 1993 to 1995, where she taught English to Swazi and Zulu children in rural schools. In addition to writing poetry, she is a translator, having recently completed the selected poems of Uruguay's Delmira Agustini. Her poetry has appeared in *The Best American Poetry 1996* (Scribner), *Parnassus, Prairie Schooner, The Bloomsbury Review,* and other journals. She is assistant professor of English at Highlands University in Las Vegas, New Mexico. Her first book, *Absence, Luminescent* won the Four Way Books Larry Levis Prize and will be published in 1999.

GLORIA VANDO's book of poems *Geography of the Impossible* (Arte Publico Press) won the 1994 Thorpe Menn Award. Her work has appeared in numerous anthologies, including *In Other Words: Literature by Latinas of the United States* (Arte Publico Press), *Looking for Home* (Milkweed Editions), and *Dog Music* (St. Martin's Press). Her honors include fellowships from the Kansas Arts Commission and the Barbara Deming Memorial Award. She is the editor of *The Helicon Nine Reader,* an anthology featuring the best of ten years of *Helicon Nine,* a journal of women's writing she founded in 1977. She is cofounder of the Writer's Place, a literary center in Kansas City, where she lives and publishes books under the Helicon Nine imprint.

ACKNOWLEDGMENTS

Grateful acknowledgment is made to the editors of the publications from which the poems in this volume were chosen.

SANDRA M. CASTILLO: "Letter to Yeni on Peering into Her Life," "Almendares," "Primos," "Monday Night at Pedro's," "The Contra," "At the Havana Hilton," "En el Sol de Mi Barrio," "Rincón," "El Apagón," and "Cuba" used by permission of the author. Copyright © 1997 by Sandra M. Castillo.

LORNA DEE CERVANTES: "An Interpretation of Dinner by the Uninvited Guest" and "Starfish" from *Emplumada*. Copyright © 1981 by Lorna Dee Cervantes. Used by permission of the University of Pittsburgh Press. "The Poet Is Served Her Papers," "The Levee: Letter to No One," and "To We Who Were Saved by the Stars" from *From the Cables of Genocide: Poems on Love and Hunger*, published by Arte Publico Press. Copyright © 1991 by Lorna Dee Cervantes. Used by permission of the author. "Isla Mujeres," "A un Desconocido," "On the Poet Coming of Age," "First Beating," and "Archeology" used by permission of the author. Copyright © 1997 by Lorna Dee Cervantes. "Isla Mujeres" appeared in *The Bloomsbury Review*. "First Beating" and "Archeology" appeared in *Many Mountains Moving*.

JUDITH ORTIZ COFER: "The Changeling," "Saint Rose of Lima," "The Purpose of Nuns," "Women Who Love Angels," "The Campesino's Lament," "Las Magdalenas," "The Lesson of the Teeth," "My Grandfather's Hat," "Anniversary," and "The Lesson of the Sugarcane" from *The Latin Deli*. Copyright © 1993 by Judith Ortiz Cofer. Used by permission of the University of Georgia Press.

VÍCTOR HERNÁNDEZ CRUZ: "Keeping Track of the Serpents," "La Milagrosa," "Two Guitars," and "Perlas" from *By Lingual Wholes*, published by Momos Press. Copyright © 1982 by Víctor Hernández Cruz. Used by permission of the author. "Snaps of Immigration," "Scarlet Skirt," and "New/Aguas Buenas/Jersey" from *Red Beans*, published by Coffee House Press. Copyright

"Nobody Here but Us," "Dangerous Hats," "Elite Syncopations," "A Diver for the NYPD Talks to His Girlfriend," "El Zapato," and "Note Folded Thirteen Ways" used by permission of the author. Copyright © 1997 by Richard García. "A Diver for the NYPD Talks to His Girlfriend" appeared in *The Bloomsbury Review.* "El Zapato" appeared in *Prairie Schooner.* "Note Folded Thirteen Ways" appeared in *The Greensboro Review* and *The Pushcart Prize: Best of the Small Presses,* published by Pushcart Press.

RAY GONZÁLEZ: "Calling the White Donkey" from *Railroad Face,* published by Chile Verde Press. Copyright © 1995 by Ray González. Used by permission of the author. "Brown Pot," "The Angels of Juárez, Mexico," "At the Rio Grande Near the End of the Century," and "Savior" used by permission of the author. Copyright © 1997 by Ray González. "At the Rio Grande Near the End of the Century" appeared in *Our Lady of the Lake Writer's Institute Anthology,* published by Our Lady of the Lake University. "Cabato," "There," "Still Life with Endings," "Beyond Having," and "Without Villages" from *Cabato Sentora.* Copyright © 1998 by Ray González. Used by permission of BOA Editions. "Beyond Having" appeared in the *Indiana Review.*

MAURICE KILWEIN GUEVARA: "The Magic Carpet," "The Buddy Holly Poem," "The Long Woman Bathing," "Tuesday Shaman," and "Abuelo, Answers and Questions" from *Postmortem.* Copyright © 1994 by Maurice Kilwein Guevara. Used by permission of the University of Georgia Press. "A Rhyme for Halloween," "The Miniaturist," "The Easter Revolt Painted on a Tablespoon," "Make-up," and "Long Distance" from *Poems of the River Spirit.* Copyright © 1996 by Maurice Kilwein Guevara. Used by permission of the University of Pittsburgh Press.

JUAN FELIPE HERRERA: "Cherry Bowl with Blue Revolver: Neo-American Landscape" from *Facegames,* published by As Is, So & So Press. Copyright © 1987 by Juan Felipe Herrera. Used by permission of the author. "The Yellow Room," "Portrait of Woman in Long Black Dress/Aurelia," and "Mexican World Mural / 5 × 25" from *Akrilica,* published by Alcatraz Editions. Copyright © 1989 by Juan Felipe Herrera. Used by permission of the author. "The Poetry of America," "Future Martyr of Supersonic Waves," "Resurrection of the Flesh," "When He Believed Himself to Be a Young Girl Lifting the Skin of the Water," "The Dream of Christopher Columbus," and "Atavistic: Traces after the Rain" used by permission of the author. Copyright © 1997 by Juan Felipe Herrera.

DIONISIO D. MARTÍNEZ: "A Discreet Prayer" and "The Death of Isadora Duncan" from *Dancing at the Chelsea*. Copyright © 1992 by Dionisio D. Martínez. Used by permission of State Street Press. "Standard Time: Novena for My Father," "Carp," and "Cole Porter" from *History as a Second Language*. Copyright © 1993 by Dionisio D. Martínez. Used by permission of Ohio State University Press. "The Cultivation of Orchids," "Kinescope," "Matisse: Blue Nude, 1952," "Nocturnes," and "Altruism" from *Bad Alchemy*. Copyright © 1995 by Dionisio D. Martínez. Used by permission of W. W. Norton.

VALERIE MARTÍNEZ: "Night of Fathers," "The Human Universe," "Tesoro," "Children of the Disappeared," "Absence, Luminescent," "The New World," "The Reliquaries," "Traveler," "It Is Not," and "Nocturne" used by permission of the author. Copyright © 1997 by Valerie Martínez. "Night of Fathers" appeared in *Parnassus: Poetry in Review*. "Tesoro," "Absence, Luminescent," "It Is Not," and "Nocturne" appeared in *Prairie Schooner*. "It Is Not" appeared in the *Best American Poetry 1996*, Scribner.

GLORIA VANDO: "In the Dark Backward," "My Mother Cunning, yet Innocent," "Commonwealth, Common Poverty," "Knife," and "Lydia's Phantasmagoria" from *Stiletto One*. Copyright © 1989 by Gloria Vando. Used by permission of the author. "Father's Day," "In the Crevices of Night," "Swallows of Salangan," "Blanca's Red Lips," and "Ode to Your Back" used by permission of the author. Copyright © 1997 by Gloria Vando. "Father's Day," "In the Crevices of Night," "Blanca's Red Lips," and "Ode to Your Back" appeared in *Cottonwood Magazine*. "Swallows of Salangan" appeared in *Western Humanities Review*.